Power Brainstorming:
Great Ideas At Lightning Speed

Power Brainstorming
Great Ideas At Lightning Speed

by

Hazel Wagner PhD

B9D, Inc.

© 2008, 2009, Hazel Wagner, PhD, B9D, Inc.

Part of the Brainiance Books series published by B9D, Inc.

All rights reserved for the entire book. Reproduction, scanning, uploading, distribution, or translation of any part of this work without permission of the publisher and author is unlawful in any form by any means and punishable by law.

Whole Brain ® and HBDI® and Walk-Around® are registered trademarks of Herrmann International and the term is used with written permission thereof. Each of the Assessments mentioned are registered trademarks of their own company.

Disclaimer: This publication is written and designed to provide businesses and individuals with techniques and tools to bring out and escalate natural creativity. The author and publisher do not assume any responsibility for errors, omissions, or diversity of interpretations, and cannot be held liable for any business results either directly or indirectly. While the author made ever effort to provide accurate Internet addresses and other resources listed at the time of publication, neither the author nor the publisher assume any responsibility for errors or omissions, or changes that occur after publication.

The characters, companies, and situations are completely fictitious and any similarities to existing companies are purely coincidental.

ISBN: 978-0-9785801-1-7

Lightning button ©iStockphoto.com/Bubaone, used with permission.

Text typeset in Adobe Minion, Papyrus and Myriad typefaces

Interior design and production by Marin Bookworks, www.marinbookworks.com

Acknowledgements

There are so many people to whom I owe thanks, who brainstormed with me on business issues, and who gave me their feedback on what was working and what could be improved. My business associates and clients tested these materials before and, again, while I was writing this book. I especially want to thank Ralf Seiffe and Gideon King for their careful and insightful comments on an early draft of the book and to Ralf for writing the foreword.

In addition to all the successes there were mistakes and times a bit off the mark that taught me. As I say in the book, if you never fail you aren't trying hard enough; you aren't stepping out of your comfort zone often enough. So thank you also to those who taught me what didn't work.

A special thank you to Laura Baker, Joel Friedlander, Ann Herrmann-Nedhi, Jim Higgins, Karen Neely Reed, Will and Claudia Bullas, Taylor Bohl, all the wonderful people I worked with at G.E. and Digital Equipment Corporation, all the clients of B9D, Inc. and all the friends and strangers who have sent me comments on my Blogs and web sites.

And of course, thank you to my family whose patience with me, while I pushed myself to extremes of sleep deprivation, meant there were times I wasn't as available to them. It's finally done!

A special thank you to my famous photographer daughter, Audrey Wancket, (www.wancketstudios.com) who did that great photo of me for the front cover.

Dedication

To My Parents, Hans and Hildegard Freeman

My parents' bravery, creativity, and intelligence got them out of Germany and into the United States during a very dangerous and difficult time. Their life and work ethics inspired me to study hard and to share with others what I learned. I proudly carry on their beliefs by sharing with you the exceptional results and innovation you can achieve through power brainstorming.

Table of Contents

Foreword
by Ralf Steiffe 11

Prologue:
Brainstorming: The Free Thinking Process 17

Chapter 1
The Brainstorming History Trail 21

Chapter 2
What do We Know About Our Brain That Will Help Us Brainstorm 27

Chapter 3
The Nitty Gritty of Brainstorming: Speed and Documentation 31

Chapter 4
Creativity, Chaos and Charting 39

Chapter 5
Use Your Whole Brain for Brainstorming 47

Chapter 6
15 Non-Rules for Brainstorming 59

Chapter 7
Critical Thinking: The Who?, What? How? Questions. 67

Chapter 8
Evaluating Critical Thinking Questions and Generating New Solutions. . . . 79

Chapter 9
Individual Brainstorming 87

Chapter 10
Go For Diversity! 95

Chapter 11
When Minds Click: Collaborative Brainstorming Power. 105

Chapter 12
Planning for a Brainstorming Session. 113

Chapter 13
Using Tools to Help Trigger Brainstorming Visual Thinking 125

Chapter 14
Mind Mapping: Mind Maps as Tools for Brainstorming 133

Chapter 15
Clustering Explained. 141

Chapter 16
The Forest, The Trees and The Flower. 149

Chapter 17
Brainstorming Card Decks 159
Chapter 18
Brainstorming With A Large Audience 167
Chapter 19
Build a Business Culture for Innovation Brainstorming 175
Chapter 20
Epilogue: What You Have Gained 185
Chapter 21
Bonus Exercises 189
Resources
Additional Material, Reading and Brainstorming Tools 193
Notes and Credits 201

Foreword

For the first time in recorded history, a large part of the planet is on the upswing in economic terms. In the last fifty years, Planet Earth has enjoyed at least three events that have had profoundly beneficial effects for human beings. The Green Revolution applied technology and chemistry to agriculture with stunning effects on world hunger. The liberalization of political systems has opened minds and markets in many formerly closed or totalitarian countries. The information age has gigantically increased productivity and brought products and services to the public while shrinking the globe in a practical sense.

The combined result of these and other developments is that we are seeing the beginning of conquering scarcity, at least for a large proportion of the globe. Certainly, there are vast numbers of people that still are in want but the speed at which developing economies are coming to parity with the "developed" world is remarkable. Every continent is enjoying long-term growth, on average, a condition unprecedented in human history. Indeed, the nations that were once the most impoverished are experiencing the greatest gains on their small economic bases.

The inevitable effect of this growth will be two-fold. First, the growing technical capabilities of the new economies will manifest as worthy competition for world and domestic markets. Their labor costs and, increasingly, their educational accomplishments will create long term comparative advantages. Collaterally, these countries will become vast markets themselves and their trading partners will be active in them.

The second effect of diminishing scarcity will be to introduce *choice* into the decision process of many new consumers. When there are more goods and services available than one can consume or can afford to consume, one has to discriminate between various choices. From the sellers' points of view, this means it is profitable to differentiate one's product from those of the competitors so that consumers see value in choosing one product over the other guy's.

This notion of choice is nothing new in the first world but as the emerging nations integrate these concepts on a large scale, they will become even more effective competitors. Their own domestic market will provide the base from which to extract profits with which to reinvest and, from that, come to equivalence with first world producers.

The obvious lesson from this analysis is that an organization's continued relevance depends on offering choices to consumers that overcome domestic and foreign competitors in a marketplace that will be characterized by increasing choice. This will put a premium on innovation and differentiation, the qualities that will attract consumer's attentions and dollars.

This concept of markets with increasing choice and differentiation is completely integrated in the U.S. economy; and enterprises seek to institutionalize the methods that create dependable innovation. Creating successful new consumer service or industrial products or writing useful software code is a daunting prospect in a market that already features a half dozen competitors that are pursuing the same customers that you have identified. This is also true in the service and non-profit sectors if the mushrooming number of banks and the expanding number of organizations seeking the donation of one's automobile is any indication.

Successful innovation comes in three flavors. There are a few blockbuster ideas that change the way markets are regarded. The Walkman˚ personal music players Sony introduced in the 1970's are just such an idea. There are enhancements that fundamentally advance an existing concept like Apple's iPod at the beginning of this century. Then there are small ideas that continually improve an existing product like much larger storage capability on these music players and different form factors for the units.

IPod owners are probably shaking the heads in disagreement about this assessment of their favorite musical device. The fact is that there were several hard-drive based mp3 players on the market before the ubiquitous white player appeared. The French company Archos had a 20 GB machine on the market long before Apple's iPod; it worked well and was easier to use than the eventual Apple system—at least for Windows˚ users.

Yet, one doubts if many of us remember the Archos product (derivatives are still on the market) because Apple followed the advice you will find in *Power Brainstorming: Great Ideas At Lightening Speed*. Whereas the French were content to stop at the first good idea (a hard drive player that could inventory the content of hundreds of cassette tapes), Apple pressed on. The result was a stunning design based on a single-track wheel is monochromatic white, rather than the usual black and chrome.

Apple didn't stop there, either. They also thought about the supply of music that would fill the iPods and came up with music management software to fill the players and a digital rights management system to please the musicians and their lawyers. The result was iTunes, an idea that *does* fit the first category of blockbuster ideas. The result is that the players have market share north of 70% and the software has propelled Apple into position as the world's largest music retailer.

The lesson here is that innovative products trump ordinary ones even if they cost more and even if the competitor has huge cost advantages. Apple created this advantage by pushing forward, past the first idea of a new but not unique music player, to a systematic approach to the whole market of mobile entertainment.

This concept of not stopping at the first idea is one of several that readers will find in *Power Brainstorming*. Others include the concept of speed when starting a brainstorming session because it eliminates self-censorship or group criticism. Can you imagine the lost opportunity if people in the Apple conference room, a company that is primarily a hardware manufacturer, turned thumbs down on the genius who first blurted out "we can control the music business and eliminate compact disks and players with software!"?

Another important idea is that of diversity. Many of us are tired of the constant attention HR pays to the concept but in *Power Brainstorming* we learn how intellectual diversity is an irreplaceable element in successful innovation. It shows why the differences in thinking styles add to the process and why folks with different thinking styles must be included and nurtured by leaders with necessarily different styles.

Regardless of one's frame of reference, be it business, service or non-profit organizations or even the government, it is necessary to find a way to create a customer experience that is unique, positive, and memorable.

What does it take to create an experience that exceeds expectations? What can the dry cleaner do that meets this aim? What can the service department do to make sure the customer returns the next time the oil needs changing? How can a mass merchandiser change its business model to remain relevant in a hyper-competitive marketplace? What new features can we invent that will "wow 'em"? Or, why will charitably minded donors pick our cause rather than another?

Managers explicitly know that the answers to these questions will determine their organization's fate and they implicitly understand that getting beyond what the customer expects is the key to continued relevance. What they may not know is how to approach the task in a systematic and repeatable way.

Hazel Wagner's years of experience as a mathematician, a teacher, a computer marketer, a global business manager, an entrepreneur and now an evangelist for systematic thinking has uniquely prepared her to present a comprehensive approach to the notion of brainstorming. This is the process of discovering new ideas, developing novel approaches and finding the best solutions. To accomplish these goals, Hazel introduces a number of concepts that explain how we perceive, that identify the different thinking patterns individuals exhibit and that illustrate how these may be usefully integrated at the organizational level.

In *Power Brainstorming*, Hazel demystifies the brainstorming process by showing how it works with the results of her own research and with support from some of the best minds on the subject. Readers will finds many practical techniques and tools such as mind mapping and clustering that position and empower individuals to take on any organization's most nettlesome problems or opportunities. She helps with rules for brainstorming (Hint: they are non-rules!) and how to plan effective brainstorming sessions.

One of the more valuable features of *Power Brainstorming* is the ongoing "case study" of a fictional group of neophyte brainstormers. Composed of archetype characters that any reader will recognize, this group is unexpectedly assembled to think about their business problems and opportunities. They illustrate some of the issues that arise when introducing brainstorming and the solutions they design show how similar concerns might crop up—and be surpassed---in one's own brainstorming sessions.

Another of this book's useful elements is the worksheets and exercises that end each chapter. Rather than simply presenting the information in what might be considered a printed lecture, *Power Brainstorming* engages the reader with relevant questions and thought experiments. Their purpose is to help solidify the information but they have a great take-away value for any readers who integrate these questions in their every day work.

Also included are software tools and links to sites that offer products and services that can help organizations considering ways to integrate the ideas that *Power Brainstorming* advocates. These are helpful, not expensive and offer varied approaches to the same goal. A recommended reading list is also appended.

*

As the elimination of scarcity becomes evident to all, it will be those who have prepared by creating innovative products and services that will best engage challengers, enter new markets and earn the largest categorical margins. Preparation starts with a systematic approach to achieve innovation that constantly produces small improvements, regularly creates significant advances and occasionally invents a blockbuster. Regular *brainstorming* inculcated into an organization is the process that will accomplish this. If you are responsible for the growth of a business or organization or even if you are simply an individual who wants to understand the theory and application of systematic, creative thought, take the time to read *Power Brainstorming: Great Ideas At Lightning Speed*. Then apply the very first lesson at work or on the worksheets. You will then have taken the first step towards preparing for a successful future.

> Ralf Seiffe
> Partner, Transmedial Communications LLC
> Institute for Truth in Accounting
> Northbrook, Illinois
> USA

Prologue

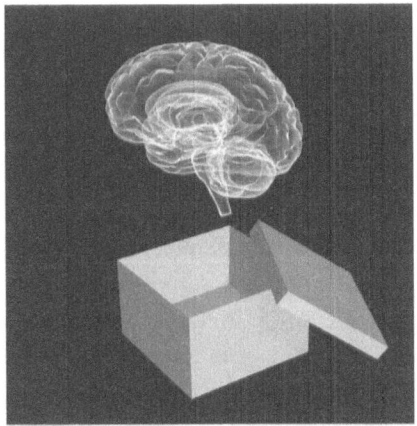

© *Jeffrey Collingwood fotolia*

Brainstorming: The Free Thinking Process

The best way to have good ideas is have lots of ideas.

I decided to write this book as I observed businesses in America grappling with ways to keep and increase their profits in a highly competitive global economy. What I have come to understand and believe is that *free-form idea generation among a company's employees and customers creates power* for that company to shoot ahead of its competitors, find new markets, solve new needs, and develop meaningful businesses.

This book will hopefully encourage you to brainstorm whenever having a number of options to consider will be better than having just one. And hopefully the book will show you why that happens much more often than you might have been thinking.

Usually, the first solution ideas are the most common, most familiar, but they may not be the best solution. This book will also dispel the myth that all there is to brainstorming is someone standing in front of the group who writes down what the group says and stops when someone says 'that is a good idea.'

The tools and techniques in this book are distilled from the hundreds of seminars and facilitations with all kinds of companies represented, from small entrepreneurial start-ups to the global top 50. I have worked with groups with a single responsibility such as customer service, and with groups with diverse responsibilities from CEO down to the receptionist -- all are represented in this book.

I come from a discipline that you would think of as the furthest career departure from creativity and brainstorming. I have a PhD in Mathematics. We tend to think that there's a linear process to solving mathematics problems and that there's probably just one correct answer to any problem. What I learned from that discipline was the importance of studying processes rather than the answer. Processes give you the ability to solve many more problems, and knowing a variety of processes or methods gives you the flexibility to solve many types of problems.

Moving into a wider world where business decisions reflect the needs of the customers and the need to generate profit made perfect sense to me. I naturally gravitated towards computer sales and loved it! That was the early 80's, just when purchasing computers became automatic for businesses. No one had personal computers at that time. IBM people wore white coats in the computer labs of their customers. The industry was "The Untouchables." You were somebody special if you worked with computers,

In school, one learns to think linearly, "How do I take the fewest number of steps to get to the answer at the back of the book?"

It was clear that the idea of linear thinking and only one answer didn't apply to the business world. The world at large - "life" - isn't like that, either. In life we make a choice between lots of options, and we make the best choices when we look at all of our options. With several choices, you can choose the criteria you care about the most to determine which option to try first. Your main concern may be return on your investment or it might be initial cost, or, it could be how it will attract a new customer base.

This sort of creative brainstorming was indeed very different from my original studies! I loved the field; it was growing by leaps and bounds and was exciting. When talking to customers my co-worker and I would brainstorm with them about the functions they needed their computers to accomplish and then bring the information back to our product developers.

After fifteen or more years in the business world, I realized that people at the top are exploring lots of ideas, but they are still looking for the one right answer.

I left Digital Equipment Corporation (DEC) to start up my own business, called B9D, which provides marketing resources for companies in technology fields who don't have a marketing mindset, or for those who feel that marketing is not the best use of their own time. My experience when engineers ran a company, they understandably thought like engineers. Companies need some people who think like their customers and know how to apply marketing and sales methods.

B9D means "Beyond 9 Dots." The name comes from the idea of thinking outside the box as in the following puzzle. If you draw three rows of three dots so that they form a box, and then connect the dots with four lines without lifting up your pencil, you have to allow your lines to go outside of the shape of the box. The natural instinct people have is to never go outside of the box. Until they realize that there is no rule that says you can't go outside of the box, they cannot connect the dots. Hence the expression "Thinking outside the box."

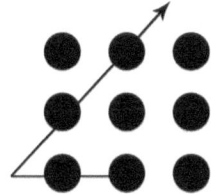

Thinking differently, being able to recognize and question your assumptions about a puzzle or problem, is an essential part of the "secret" to making money in today's world.

As a professional speaker; business brainstorming has been a major subject of my speeches and seminars for the last 10 years. I want to share as much as I can of that experience, with you, in this book. I have included a practice section at the end of each chapter, so that by the end of the book, you and your team will have the tools to consistently generate unique options for every business challenge. And I do mean every challenge. Brainstorming is a tool that allows you to come up with better options and solutions of all kinds

I hope that you will recognize that you've been brainstorming all along, but will now be able to do it more often and better. My second hope is that you now realize that this is a businesslike thing to do. Brainstorming isn't just for the artsy people at the other side of the building with portfolios of graphics and drawings; it's for the accountants, administrators, coders, customer service technicians and…the customers.

Every part of a business is open to brainstorming – this is a business skill that maintains and expands profitability by opening all of the doors and windows, creating skylights, drilling new basements and routinely knocking down walls. It's radical and fun, and the biggest "rule" is that there are no rules.

This book is for the business manager who wants to incorporate brainstorming into the company as an important way to generate new profits through employee creativity.

It is also for the individual who wants to systematically approach the problems in his or her life with a planned creative process.

Initially, a business manager might ask, "Who can afford to implement brainstorming across the board?" As you read and realize the enormous profit potential that brainstorming presents, I think your question will change to, "Who can afford NOT to implement brainstorming company-wide?"

People are a company's greatest asset – especially if those people are skilled at generating new and creative options and solutions.

A 'storm a day keeps competitors at bay.

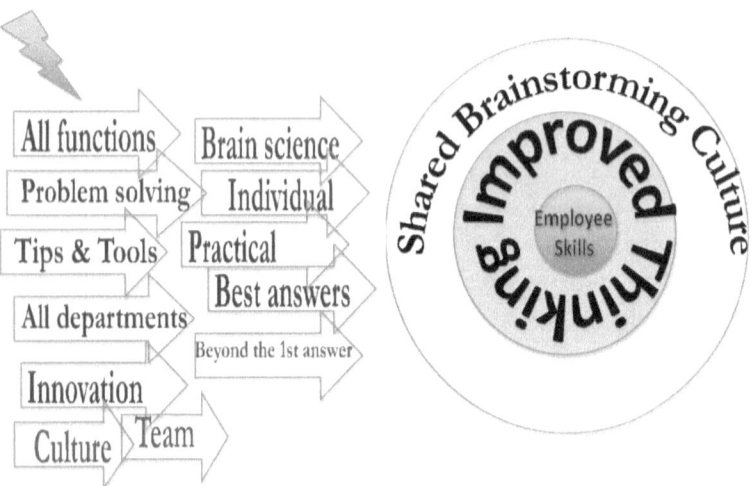

Chapter 1

The Brainstorming History Trail

"Those that fail to learn from history are doomed to repeat it."

— ATTRIBUTED TO BOTH GEORGE SANTAYANA
AND WINSTON CHURCHILL

© *Stephen Coburn - Fotolia.com*

Alex Osborn (1888-1966), suddenly without a job, took clippings of his published news stories and showed them to the city editor of a rival newspaper. He was told the articles weren't very good, but each contained an idea. So the editor took a chance and hired him. Osborn started to think how important an idea could be, that ideas were actually valued and made a resolution to start thinking up and writing down ideas every day 'like a boy scout doing one good turn every day.'

Osborn went on to write many books on creativity, coin the word *brainstorming*, and start the immensely successful advertising firm BBDO (Barton, Batten, Durstine & Osborn).

"Whatever creative success I gained was due to my belief that creative power can be stepped up by effort, and that there are ways in which we can guide our creative thinking." Alex Osborn said in his book, Your *Creative Power*. Osborn believed that 'drive' was a part of creativity, that a person must want to come up with ideas, should exercise his or her imagination and that they could improve through practice.

According to Osborn, creativity and ideas can come from invention, discovery, or association. Three of his observations and definitions:

1. Invention is something new, not seen or known before. For example: a plastic holder that can be held in the mouth for x-rays.[1]
2. Discovery means that the idea was not known to you or in the context or application. For example: lasers to permanently remove hair.
3. Association is putting known ideas together in a new combination. Applying a rolling ball that applies deodorant to dispensing ink from a pen.

All three resulted in new and profitable applications.

To accomplish any of the three takes experience, knowledge, openness to explore and express ideas that come to mind, sharing ideas with others and discussing them as possibilities.

Brainstorming: What is it?

Brainstorming is a method of forcing your brain (and others taking part in a group session) to think and express ideas so *fast* that the rest of your brain doesn't have time to censor. Words and ideas can come tumbling out one after another, each one creating a connection to more words and ideas. Pictures and associations flash through your mind, and if you document them as they come with no regard to what makes sense, you will find the results filled with options and new connections that will lead to new ways of thinking about a subject, multiple options for solutions of problems, and loads of ideas to be investigated and considered. Wow! Then what?

Actually we do brainstorming internally all the time, in little short bursts. Too often we don't write down an idea that sounded fantastic at the time and later can't remember it. Other times we remember, but we start censoring and telling ourselves, "Aw that won't work" or "Others will tell me it's a stupid idea." And that can be a great loss to you and your company, because the germ of an idea can often be the trigger to bring on many more great ideas or be combined in some way to produce the perfect answer you were looking for.

Why Start (or Do More) Brainstorming?

Break out of old habits to achieve new, creative, different, fun and breakthrough results and especially to push past the first ideas to get to the best ideas. To find great ideas you need lots and lots of good, mediocre and bad ideas. A large number of ideas even if they aren't all good in themselves, spawn many more ideas and amongst the many will surface some great ones.

To solve problems on which you may be stuck. you need to be trying different methods.

> *"Productive work is the process ...of translating an idea into physical form"* and *"all work is creative work if done by a thinking mind"*
>
> ~ *John Galt speaking in* Atlas Shrugged
> *by Ayn Rand*

When to brainstorm?

Brainstorm whenever having a number of options to consider will be better than having just one.

When facing a situation or problem it may seem natural to jump up and get started the moment you have *one solution*. This attitude may have come from spending years taking tests in school where there was only one right answer. Real life and business situations most often have many options. Only after forcing yourself or the group to keep thinking of more options, even after you have a solution, will you have a number of solutions so that you can weigh the relative merits of each option to pick one to apply.

The first solution ideas that will come to mind are the most common, most familiar, but they may not be the best solution. Only when you have looked at as many ideas as you can come up with in the allotted time (and sometimes this may be short as in some emergency situations) can you weigh the benefits of each and feel that you came up with a better solution or at least one you feel more confidence in than if you had taken the first thing that popped into someone's mind.

Scheduling the Brainstorm Group Session

Osborn believed that you had to plan time for thinking. You need quiet time in a place where you could think without interruption. John C. Maxwell in *Thinking for a Change* advocates the same process. Both feel you have to make appointments in your calendar for yourself, for just thinking and making notes of ideas you generate.

A 'Storm a Day

It is essential for businesses to brainstorm nearly every day. In a changing world, businesses face both problems and opportunities that make flexibility instead of rigidity into a great advantage. Flexibility asks, "What are the options open to us?" The business that wants to be innovative discovers and solves problems before their competitors even see them on the horizon. These businesses can use brainstorming techniques for a better ROI of their time spent.

Sharing Your Ideas

Once you've generated ideas, share them. At times it takes courage to express your ideas. Sometimes you might be afraid that others will not like your ideas or might even laugh at them. It also takes courage to overcome your own self-doubt. There is no more important role for a manager to take than being a creative coach, an encourager of anyone with suggestions and ideas to improve the business, products, or services.

YOUR PERFECT STORM

Think of one business problem you are facing and on a separate piece of paper complete this sentence 20 times within five minutes: What if we/I . . . ?

Now, answer the following question using just the last five (of the 20 you wrote) of the above sentence:

How would this affect the company?

Next, answer this next question using the same last five renditions of the first sentence:

How would this affect the customer?

Take your ideas and share them with at least one other person.

"A recent McKinsey Global Survey shows that companies are satisfied, overall, with their use of metrics to assess innovation portfolios — though many findings suggest that they shouldn't be."
~ *McKinsey Quarterly* November, 2008:

Chapter 2

What do We Know About Our Brain That Will Help Us Brainstorm?

"The brain is a wonderful organ; it starts working the moment you get up in the morning and does not stop until you get into the office"

— ROBERT FROST (1874 - 1963)

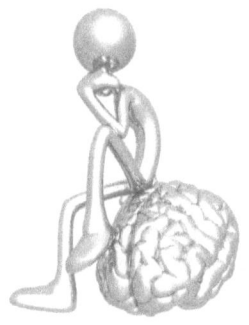

© Scott Maxwell - Fotolia.com

We humans have made plenty of mistakes trying to figure out our own brain. At one time it was thought that we needed to understand our brain in order to build a computer to emulate it. Then we thought we could learn from how computers work to understand how our brain works.

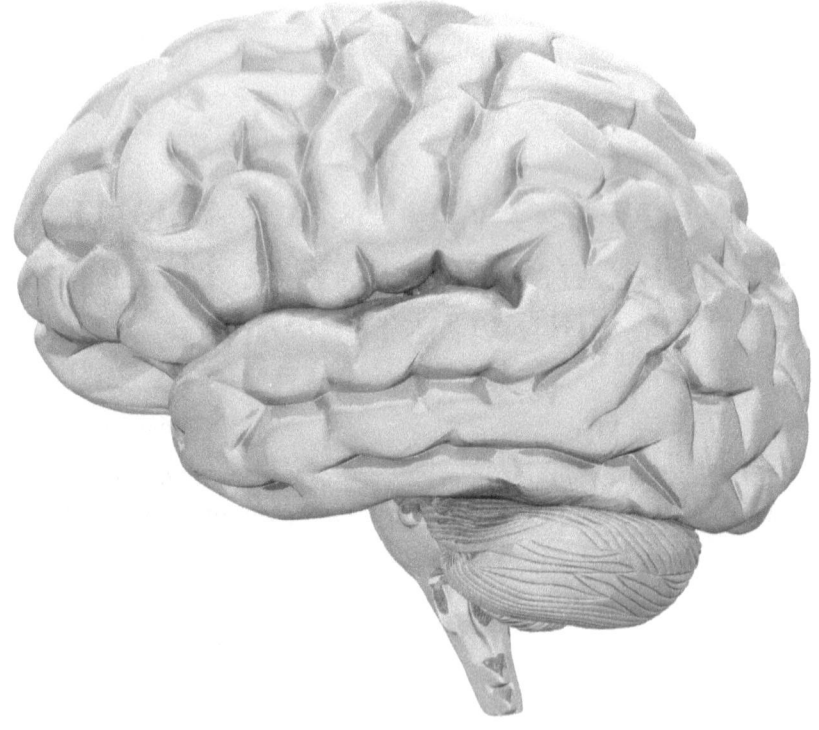

© gehirn von der seit-fotolia

Aristotle was famous for knowing everything. He taught that the brain exists merely to cool the blood and is not involved in the process of thinking. This is true only of certain persons.

~ William Jacob "Will" Cuppy (August 23, 1884 – September 19, 1949) an American humorist and literary critic,

Of all the brilliant minds that were or are still alive in my lifetime, I am most in awe of Albert Einstein. His combination of creativity and immense scientific understanding was amazing. According to Wikipedia, "Grey matter, the thin layer of cells covering the cerebrum, was believed by most scholars to be the primary center of cognitive and conscious processing. White matter, the mass of glial cells that support the cerebral gray matter, was assumed to primarily provide nourishment, physical support, and connective pathways for the more functional cells on the cerebral surface. But research fueled by the interest of Dr. Marian Diamond in the glial structure of Albert Einstein's brain led to a line of research that offered strong evidence that glial cells serve a computational role beyond merely transmitting processed signals between more functional parts of the brain. In 2004, *Scientific American* published an article suggesting scientists in the early 21st century are only beginning to study the 'other half of the brain.'

> *When I examine myself and my methods of thought, I come close to the conclusion that the gift of fantasy has meant more to me than my talent for absorbing positive knowledge.*
>
> ~Albert Einstein

When we brainstorm we are both following connections that already exist in our brain and creating new ones. Research done on Einstein's brain after his death seems to indicate that it is the number and complexity of the connections that are different. His brain was no different in size or weight from others.

> *To invent, you need a good imagination and a pile of junk.*
>
> ~Thomas A. Edison (1847 - 1931)

YOUR PERFECT STORM

You are operating 10 coin Laundromats and six carwashes in your city. Lately, profits have fallen off from these enterprises. Use the following words to create a new way of marketing these businesses to consumers. Come up with at least three ways that could work.

Hot dog	Razor
Spine	Joy
Duvet	Murder

Chapter 3

The Nitty Gritty of Brainstorming: Speed and Documentation

"In quickness is truth."

– Ray Bradbury, American author of more than 500 articles and books

© *kreego - Fotolia.com*

Images, ideas, words, phrases rapidly tumble out, each creating multiple connections, each flashing signals from different parts of the human brain, allowing seemingly random connections to begin to cohere as a whole, as a meaningful image, thought, or idea. Or, if done in a group, the group creates scaffolding on the 'knowing' of other brains, which generates directions that, without this process, would never have occurred.

In the 1970's, companies (especially in the U.S.) started to realize the importance of creativity and innovation. Edward De Bono wrote about "lateral thinking," Tony Buzan coined the word and popularized "mind mapping," and Gabriele Rico developed "clustering." The last two processes allowed individuals to brainstorm, spilling onto the page whatever ideas and images popped into their minds. These methods of ideation, mind mapping and clustering, have been taking a long time to move into mainstream business thinking.

Human beings can think much faster than they can talk, and they can talk faster than they can write. Our brains can go faster than we can tell someone our ideas. For instance, if you had to think at the pace that people were talking, you would go to sleep from boredom. On the other hand, the brain works so quickly, that we cannot normally capture all of the ideas zooming through it. So when we allow ourselves to talk or write closer to the speed that the brain actually works, then we generate electricity, and ideas pour out willy-nilly.

Self-confidence in Solving Problems

Here is a brainstorming method you can easily try the next time you have a group together. In my brainstorming seminars, we do "brain writing," where a group at a table receives a piece of paper divided into columns or rows, and I give them a question or problem relevant to their business. They see 24 spaces on the paper. I then tell the participants to write down three solutions going across and pass the sheet to the next person, and so forth: No repeats, no asking for more paper. The people in the group start having to write fast. They have to read quickly what's on the paper. They can't have repeats, but what's there triggers them to come up with more ideas. No names are allowed, so no one judges another person. Many of the ideas generated in this way have real value. Gradually, I see decision-makers and general employees alike accept that it makes sense to go ahead and spill out all the ideas, no matter how crazy they may sound at first.

At the end of the process, participants are shocked at what they've accomplished in a short period of time. A sense of possibility and self-confidence dawns on them and they become more open to trying the next exercise. When they're on their own the next day, because they're believers, they will use the methods that they learned. They will force themselves to brainstorm fast and come up with lots of ideas. I have to convince people that it is quantity that gives quality. You can either sift through and find the gems or create combinations that are unusual but work well or both.

Searching for Meaning and Patterns...and then Writing It All Down

The formal word is *ideation* — what the human brain does when it is searching for patterns of meaning. The informal word is *brainstorming*.

Too often we don't write down our ideas at the time and later can't remember them; ideation is ephemeral. Here are some other common definitions you will need as you read this book.

Mind mapping –A method of diagramming various ideas and their relationships to one another on paper. Mind mapping is more than just a brainstorming method, though it is a fantastic method. Mind mapping is a learning method, so you learn quicker and it's easier to recall what you learned. Mind mapping helps you gain clarity on a subject. It is a tool that allows you to sell, explain or organize a speech, so it flows and you don't have to read it word-for-word. Mind mapping helps you take notes so efficiently that you won't miss parts of a lecture, and it is a method to get all the ideas down when you are brainstorming in a group.

Mind maps can be used to organize the results of brainstorming or be the method you use to draw out more ideas as you are brainstorming.

Below are two simple mind maps, one that is a forest (big picture mind map) and one that is a 'trees' (detailed picture) mind map. These are just examples so that you can start to recognize mind maps. Later, you will learn how to use and build your own maps. The words are the keys to a larger idea, and each person's keywords can be different. The branches are the associations and connections between the words.

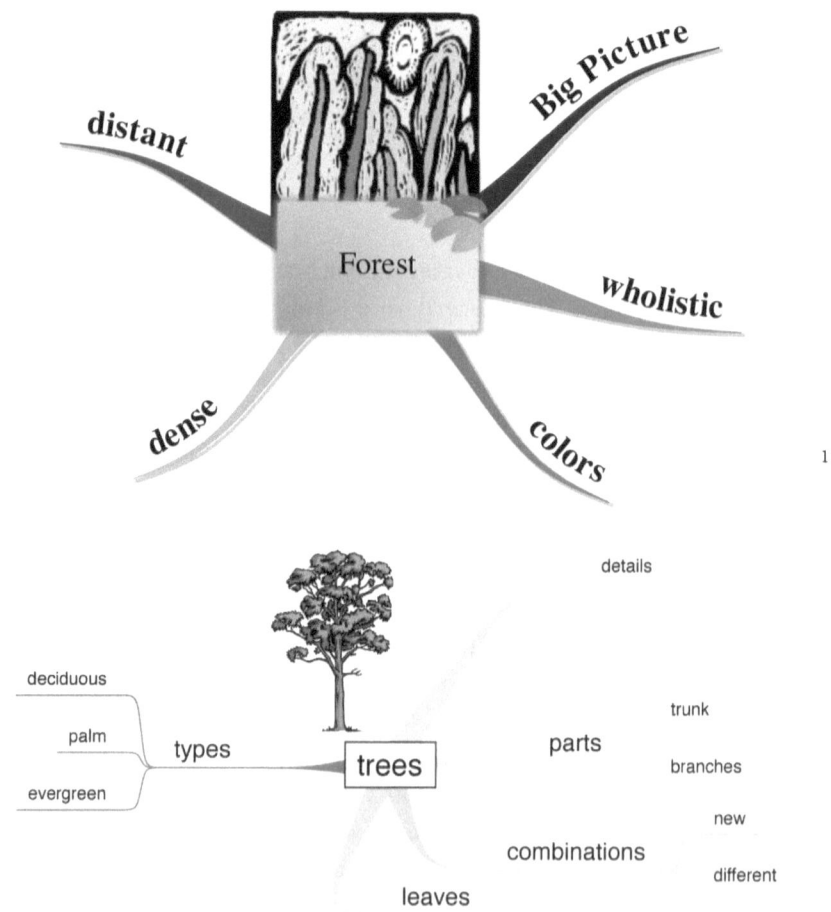

Clustering — taking the results of a brainstorming session that are usually in a list or randomly written, and grouping the ideas into related categories such as food references, fight metaphors or scientific references. You decide how to pursue as many of the most promising ideas as quickly as possible, but don't throw away the remaining ideas. You may find you want to come back and go through them every once in a while, and you may find some gems you missed the first time around.

developed using free form in ConceptDraw® www.conceptdraw.com

The Brainstorm Setting

It helps to do brainstorming in an environment that is conducive to thinking out loud (though I will explain shortly why we do a short, silent first stage), thinking fast, and documenting all the ideas and words.

Brainstorming can be done alone, with just one or two others, or with a slightly larger group. If the group gets too large it isn't possible for everyone to be participating and getting everything written down so there are some special methods to use if you find you are going to work with a very large group, such as connected laptops, slides and teams of facilitators.

In some companies 'let's brainstorm it!' only means that someone is going to stand up at a flipchart or white board and say, "OK, let's start brainstorming. Who's got an idea?" Then they look around to see if anyone is ready to speak up. Sometimes there is someone, sometimes not. Doing brainstorming the same old way every time, even if it is a good method, will become stale and boring. And worst of all, it won't get the flow of ideas started.

A definition of insanity: Doing things the same way you have always done them and expecting a different result.

Idea generation needs some mental electricity to start flowing. It has to have an accepting environment where all ideas are welcomed and noted. No one should have to think over an idea before expressing it because they worry it will be ridiculed or dismissed.

"Man's mind stretched to a new idea never goes back to its original dimensions."
~Oliver Wendell Holmes

Acknowledging 'Stormers as a Group

It is also valuable to consider the results of team brainstorming as a joint product or solution because the process encourages and works best when ideas piggyback or connect. It is the combining and trying different versions of things someone else said that helps the process grow and succeed. It is important that there is a feeling of accomplishment for each person in the group and that thanks and rewards, especially psychic rewards, go to the group as a whole.

It's Not Over…

After a brainstorming session it is important for everyone to carry around a recorder or a small pad to write on because the process just gets started with the formal team brainstorming. The brain keeps on running and thinking about the subject. Great ideas will pop into your mind and everyone's mind after they leave.

We always think we will remember because it is such a great idea but the truth is as soon as we are onto something else we forget. So write every idea down even if it seems silly or trivial at the moment. Leonardo da Vinci and Alex Osborn were known to always have a little notebook to write ideas.

Keep a pad of paper, pen, and small light or flashlight next to your bed. Ideas will come from dreams and sometimes even wake you up. Again, you won't remember them in the morning if you don't jot them down. Dreams are a fertile source of creativity because the usual limits we put on ourselves are gone. Unusual and new connections are possible and seem normal. David Kahn, a professor at Harvard Medical School, was quoted in *Parade* magazine 10/28/2008 as saying," The waking mind is thinking inside the box; the dreaming mind is thinking outside the box." Accustom yourself to keeping a record of ideas that strike you as somehow worth exploring.

YOUR PERFECT STORM

Here is a great way to quickly brainstorm a specific question if you have four or more people who can work on it. Form two groups of two to four people. Decide on a problem that needs a unique solution.

One person in each group needs to use his cell phone to record (or dial their office voicemail) the ideas that their group generates as they walk.

Go outside of your office building. Group A should begin walking rapidly around the building clockwise. While walking, each person should think of 10 possible solutions for the problem and say them into the phone.

Group B should begin walking rapidly around the building counter-clockwise and perform the same way.

Be creative here if it's raining. Remember you can use the memo feature on your cell phone instead of making an actual call. You can also use a hand-held digital recorder.

Return to the inside of the building and record each idea from the phone messaging system. Expand on the ideas that were recorded.

CHAPTER 4

CREATIVITY, CHAOS AND CHARTING

*"There are those who look at things the way they are,
and ask why...
I dream of things that never were, and ask why not?"*

- ROBERT FRANCIS KENNEDY,
1968 PRESIDENTIAL CAMPAIGN

Higher Learning
by Will Bullas, with permission of the artist. www.willbullas.com

We are all capable of so much more creativity than most of us are willing to acknowledge. We started out life comfortably using any color and scribbled any way that felt good. Only when parents or teachers told us that grass had to be green and we had to color inside the lines did we question our design.

The people who come to my brainstorming seminars are from all kinds of companies. They often have problems to solve around marketing. I find that they have been doing their marketing in the same way for years: buying ads not getting return, etc. So I say, "Let's turn it around. If you were a potential customer for your business, what sort of things are you going to pay attention to?" They start listing lots of things that happen to a customer during a day: kids, buses, looking out the window at work, and so forth. They throw out lots of ideas and come up with silly things like, "sit on the toilet" and "read a magazine." More and more ideas go down on paper and pretty soon, they realize that they have gained access to how their customer thinks.

At the end of the exercise, I say, "Now let's go back to the list and see how many of those potential customers you are reaching with a message." We discover that it is a small percentage. With the creative ideas they generated they can better decide where and how they would get a message out effectively.

Another question I'll ask is, "What are the messages that people even care about?" I come up with a number that I want them to reach – a number that sounds impossible. If people think 12 is a reasonable number of possible messages to come up with, I will ask for 50 because the first things are the same-old, same-old. I keep asking, "What else? What else?" People are forced to think more creatively and think of things that aren't the standard stuff.

I'll ask, "How many ways are there to get to work from home?"

First, they might say, "Drive," and I'll ask,

"What else?"

They might say, "Public transportation, helicopter, balloon, donkey."

I'll respond, "And if you did drive, how many different ways could you drive?"

Their answer is, "Take the highway, take surface streets, drive to the train station and take the train from there, pick up some co-workers and drive in together, stop and see a client on the way instead of going right to the office."

This sort of interchange goes on and on.

When we finish, they have often come up with a combination of things like a little balloon, for instance, with an ad on it's side and floating two feet off the sidewalk.

Now businesses are realizing how important creativity is to their long-term success. 'Me too' companies can only compete on price, and that is not a long-term strategy. Companies, such as IBM, have had programs for years in which they funded certain people (Fellows) to work on whatever they wanted, with the hope and expectation that their creativity would eventually lead to some things that might result in revenue generating innovations for the company.

> *Two roads diverged in a wood, and I--*
> *I took the one less traveled by,*
> *And that has made all the difference.*
>
> ~ Robert Frost, The Road Not Taken
> U.S. poet (1874 - 1963)

What else is creativity?

- New ideas
- New connections between old ideas
- Seeing something old in a new way
- Seeing the same thing someone else sees but seeing it differently
- Creating change
- Thinking differently
- Seeing lots of options/possibilities
- Seeing a painting as art while another just sees color on a canvas
- Seeing or creating ambiguity, which is not always comfortable
- Being willing to fail, and learning from what didn't work

> *If I find 10,000 ways something won't work, I haven't failed. I am not discouraged, because every wrong attempt discarded is another step forward.*
>
> ~ Thomas A. Edison, Encyclopedia
> Britannica, U.S. inventor (1847 - 1931)

Never failing means not trying hard enough, not testing your boundaries,. Learning what doesn't work requires that you take some risks.

Chaos Theory Applied to Brainstorming

Chaos Theory describes a system or situation in which an initial cause creates an effect that creates more effects, and so on. This is sometimes called the "butterfly effect", which is described as an eventual storm that could have been started by the air movement of a butterfly flapping its wings miles and miles away. Remember this is a theory, a mathematical theory that can be duplicated in a computer program but not proven in real life…that is, except in a great brainstorming session.

Chaos Theory attempts to explain how seemingly unpredictable, complex, and "messy" events can coalesce into interesting and useful patterns and results. Chaos theory in brainstorming allows that many directions and apparently unrelated ideas can coalesce into patterns and results that will apply and be useful in your business.

Use chaos theory as you unreservedly explore ideas in a number of directions and then look for patterns or clusters of ideas on which to focus.

In brainstorming, especially when in a group, one person's idea can create many different directions of thought processes, each one resulting in a multitude of ideas worth trying out. When you find your brainstorming results have gone in many potentially fruitful directions, you may want to divide them up and assign them to different teams or work on them one at a time.

Like most people in the business world, the group that we'll be following throughout the book is fairly new to the world of brainstorming. In the beginning, they follow a process they learned by word-of-mouth. Later, they begin to use formalized brainstorming methods from a trained facilitator. As we progress through this book, we'll see how this group advances in its ability to use brainstorming techniques to revolutionize its large coffee shop franchise corporation based in the Southeast United States. This is a fictitious company and any similarities to existing companies are purely coincidental.

 STORM NUMBER ONE

Participants

Miles Skipes – Big picture man. Account Manager in Marketing. Thirty-three years old, likes driving fast in cars and boats and going deep-sea fishing in Florida with his brothers (six). Single, never engaged.

Julia Tesser – Rational, bottom line woman. Supervisor of Telecommunications Department. Fifty-seven years old. Likes going to psychic fairs, studying astronomy and breeding Yorkshire terriers. Married to a younger man who runs an East Indian import store.

G.Q. – Detailed, organized guy. Longtime employee in Customer Service. Forty-nine years old. Goes to Revolutionary War reenactments, reads historical fiction non-stop, smokes cigarettes and eats large quantities of candied cashews. Married four times, now to his high school girlfriend, Shelia who cuts hair and only reads the funnies.

Anthony – Wants to know who cares and why they care and how they will be affected. Technical Writer for Software division. Twenty-seven years old. Independent. Rides his bike to work, blogs on bio-fuels, open relationships and US wineries, which he systematically visits, each summer.

Amy Ann Wainthrop – Facilitator. Twenty-three years old. Receptionist. Has a 15' x 8' painting she did of purple roses occupying most of her living room. Studied Marine biology in college, did her field work in Alaska. Could not decide what sort of work to pursue and became a temp when her father stopped supporting her.

*

"Excuse me?" Amy Ann Wainthrop looked up from a close inspection of her handbag's interior. "You want me to do *what*?"

Miles Skipes leaned in towards the young, blond receptionist slightly, "We need you to be a Facilitator for our brainstorming session."

Amy Ann pulled a mirror out of the cavernous interior and looked him in the eye. "I don't know that I'm qualified as a receptionist to facilitate brainstorming. What's involved?"

Miles shrugged, "You have to write down everything we say…but just keywords," he added as her eyebrows shot up. "It's no big deal, really. Like, for instance, I say 'hotdog on a stick' and you write 'hotdog' and 'stick.'"

"Is that all I have to do?"

"Yes, pretty much."

"When?"

"In thirty minutes, at 2 P.M. in the Double Mocha room. Sarina from HR is using the Latte conference room and Triple Shot is full of boxes."

Amy Ann nodded into her mirror where she was carefully inspecting the small diamond inset in her left nostril.

At 1:55 p.m., the door to Double Mocha opened and Julia Tesser, a woman who had the fortune or misfortune of looking exactly like Julia Childs seated herself gracefully in the eastern corner. Right behind came G.Q., a thin-lipped, pale man with, glasses, out-of-season sweater vest, khakis, short riding boot type shoes and the strangely unwrinkled skin of a nicotine addict.

"Are we just sitting where we want or in a circle around the table?" G.Q. asked as he settled snugly against the right side of the conference table.

"This corner is supposed to be best for communicating if you're a double Capricorn like me," Julia explained.

"Oh." G.Q. pretended to be reading the remnants from the last meeting on the board. He found such things rather silly and useless.

"Hi guys!" Miles blew in with Amy Ann in tow, his smile broadcasting hopes of more gatherings with Amy in the future. This was a start - a walk down the hall, and an entrance into a conference room. Tomorrow - maybe a walk to the car and perhaps an entrance into Manuel's for drinks.

"We only need Anthony now," Julia pointed out just as a white blond head rounded the corner and presented itself along with round spectacles and cherub blue eyes.

"I hope I didn't hold anyone up." Anthony set a bottle of Pellegrino (sparkling water) down and inspected each member.

"Amy, do you need a pad and pen?" Julia darted out of the room without waiting for an answer and returned instantly with the items. Amy Ann held these without interest.

"So, I just write down what you say?"

"Yes," Julia nodded. "We're going to go around the room, and each person has one minute to call out an idea. We're going to go around the room 20 times."

"Twenty?" Amy Ann look aghast.

"You see, Amy," Miles interjected, in what he hoped was a masterful manner, "the faster we go and the longer we go, the better the ideas."

G.Q. pointed out, "According to my timer, we have 21 minutes left."

Anthony laughed, "So, Amy are you clear?"

She nodded, "Yes."

Anthony stood up, raised his miniature green glass bottle high and said, "Let the storm begin!"

He wrote on the board, "If I was a little child, I would want to eat "blank" for lunch at the coffee shop (and mommy would want to buy it for me.)"

Then he turned to the group and yelled, "Candy!"

Amy Ann quickly jotted this down, her eyebrows knit together in growing interest.

Julia shot out, "M&Ms with trail mix!"

G.Q.: "Melon balls."
Miles: "Wieners on a stick."
Anthony: "Cake."
Julia: "Pb and j."
G.Q.: "Popcorn."
Miles: "Tater tots."

At the end of 30 minutes, Amy, with direction from Miles and Julia, drew a detailed "map" of the results grouped into these four categories:

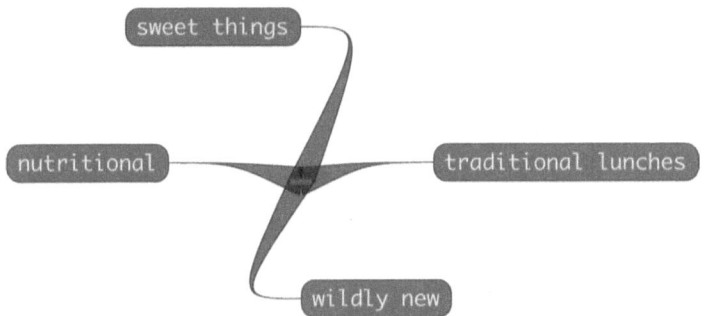

The group walked out with watermelon and miniature chocolate chip melee, broccoli slaw with honeyed pecans and Vienna sausage egg rolls with cheese dipping sauce.

"Well," Miles was at Amy Ann's elbow as she returned to her post. "What did you think of our brainstorming session?"

"I think," said Amy Ann as she settled before her computer and began to type into the Google search field, "that I want to know more about brainstorming."

Miles laughed and loitered near her bent head for a few more minutes. "OK, well, I see you're already on it. I'll talk to you later."

"Ciao," Amy Ann smiled sweetly at him. "Maybe I'll see you out on the Spiced Chai balcony at lunch sometime."

"Maybe," Miles grinned. "I'll be there tomorrow." His new leather shoes slid along the carpet as he walked away."

Amy Ann leaned back in her chair. "Ahh. I see." Her diamond stud caught the sun from the skylight. She picked up her cell phone and pushed a speedial number. "Mom? Hey. Hey listen, tell Daddy I've been practically promoted to Facilitator here. Yeah. I think it could go perm."

YOUR PERFECT STORM

In the next five minutes do one of the exercises below:

1. Describe a way to have won World War II using potatoes only but not as missiles or object weapons.

   Fearlessly share your idea with two other people, writing down their responses.

2. You have gold paint, millions of oatmeal/raisin cookies and a pair of red velvet curtains that are 11 feet long. Describe how you are going to use these items to generate $100,000 within 30 days.

3. Pick some project or problem you've been working on and write all the reasons it won't work. Make sure you have at least 12. Then take each reason and rewrite it as a reason it will work or how it will work.

Chapter 5

Use Your Whole Brain for Brainstorming

"... diversity will impact the meaning we each have behind the words that we use."

FROM ARTICLE *MAKING PARTNERSHIPS AND ALLIANCES REALLY WORK* BY NED HERRMANN

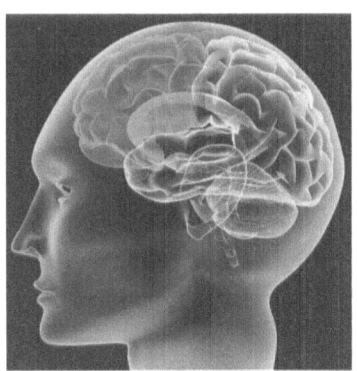

© V. Yakobchuk - Fotolia.com

Tremendous amounts of research starting with Carl Jung, and resulting in dozens of 'assessments,' have proven that we all have a preferred way of dealing with the world around us. This preferred way or cluster of attributes is sometimes described as dominance in one part of our brain. Whether it is dominance, as in Herrmann Brain Dominance Instrument®[1], type as in Myers-Briggs Type Indicator™, or style as found in a number of the assessments available, all the different kinds of test results lead to the conclusion that we aren't using all parts of our brain equally.

The term, "whole brain" refers to using all of the different parts of the brain to generate new ideas. You can do this by assembling a diverse group of people who all think using different parts of their brain, or you can do this by stimulating the different areas of your own brain with specific questions. For example, here are questions that are typical of four distinct thinking styles[2]:

Why are we doing this?   **Rational thinking style**
What is our vision?   **Experimental/big picture thinking style**
Who will be impacted?   **Interpersonal thinking style**
How and when must steps be taken?   **Organized/safekeeping thinking style**

Human thinking is almost entirely a combination of several brain tasks. For example, though the left hemisphere can read text, it takes the right hemisphere to put it into context. Mathematics is a left hemisphere function but spatial understanding, which is necessary for geometry and other parts of mathematics, requires the right hemisphere. Recognizing facial expressions requires many different parts of the brain: emotion that is in the primal inner 'reptilian' part of the brain, context in the right hemisphere, and memory in the hippocampus.[3]

Thinking Styles

The research into thinking style differences has led to the popularization of the differences between being "left brained" or "right brained." It has also led to a myriad of assessment tools[4] to determine which of four quadrants of your brain dominates your thinking or which of 16 types (e.g., Myers-Briggs[5]) describes your personality.

As the research also shows, types of thinking differences make a big impact on the brainstorming process. So big in fact that we can use these style differences as a way to create diversity when forming a brainstorming team.

In addition, when you need to brainstorm alone or when your team is small and very much alike in thinking styles, you can use the alternate styles or types to seek out more diverse ideas. For the purpose of applying our whole brain, we can use some of the differences and the types of questions each thinking style represented is more likely to ask.

Let's divide the thinking styles into four quadrants as done with HBDI®[6] A, B, C, and D.

A	D
Rational	**Experimental/ Big picture**
What's the Bottom line, just the facts?	What will the result look like?
What needs to get done?	Why are we doing this?
How much risk?	Who will benefit?
How do we get on with it?	How many options are available?
B	**C**
Safekeeping, organized	**Interpersonal**
What's the bottom line - data, proof?	How do we build the right team?
What details, what reduces risk?	Who should be on the team?
How and when must steps be taken?	Who will be impacted?

[7]

If you think back to the brainstorming team of Julia, Anthony, Miles, G.Q. and Amy Ann, Julia generally falls into the A or Rational quadrant. G.Q. falls into the B or Organized quadrant, Miles into the D or Experimental and Anthony into C or Interpersonal quadrant. Amy Ann is the Facilitator and we will see that she is a combination of Rational and Experimental.

If you have used any of the common thinking style assessments, you have a good idea about your own preferences. For example, I have a combination rational and experimental thinking style, but I continually train myself to use whole brained thinking.

Thinking Style Assessments Teach You about Yourself

The more we recognize the differences in how others think, the more open we can be in accepting those differences. This diversity of thinking leads to creativity and innovation in business. When we have an open mind to really listen, we hear ideas that would not normally register.

The next step, after opening our mind to accept and listen carefully to different ideas and methods, is to step into the shoes of people whose dominant thinking is different.

It's like walking around a pedestal that is holding your question or problem and viewing it from many angles.

Try on a Different Pair of Shoes

Sometimes you have to work on an issue or problem yourself or with only one or two others. Sometimes you may even find that a team, small or large is made up of people whose styles are very much alike. For example, they might all display predominantly Rational style. What do you do?

You can use the quadrant chart above and start asking the listed questions as if you had a different thinking style. You step into that style's shoes and act as if you are a person with that thinking style. Wear the different styles as if you were putting on a different pair of shoes.

Play the part. Think of someone who is a strong example of that style and ask the questions you know they would ask. Look at the issue or problem as they might view it. Write down everything you come up with and then take a short break, put on the next hat and go through the process again with another thinking style.

Learn to use whole brain thinking to expand your brainstorming, creativity, critical thinking, and problem solving brainstorming. The objective is to first increase options and then make choices.

Here is an example of the differences between how the styles might approach a question:

"How can I get everyone in the company to read the monthly newsletter?

A Rational answer would be: "Make the material more concise and give them facts they can use."

An Organized answer would be: "Include information on planning that they can use in their job."

A Big Picture answer would be: "Use plenty of color, pictures, and creativity."

An Interpersonal answer would be: "Have each issue include a story about one employee's hobby or charity work."

How Mind Maps Address Our Different Thinking Styles

Mind mapping of different thinking styles shows how each type participates in brainstorming sessions. One style tends to focus on the bottom line, the facts, the keywords and key ideas. They prefer to skip the details, move fast, and get to a conclusion or completion as quickly as possible.

The process of mind mapping to get everyone focused on the keywords and ideas and not get mired in details fits the Rational style. Rational thinking types are good at reminding the group of the purpose of the meeting and not to go off on a tangent. In a sense, the bottom line is always there in the middle of the screen or page. Their expression might be to stay focused and any decision is better than no decision. In our example group, Amy Ann's thinking style is predominantly Rational.

An Organized thinking style also goes for the bottom line, but in a slightly different way. An Organized thinker wants the data, the proof, all necessary details and stability. For them the fact that each subtopic can be broken out into as much detail as necessary, as long as only the keyword is written, satisfies their need to be clear about the details. Their expression might be "the devil is in the details." This style describes G.Q., the history buff, who regularly attends Civil War reenactments and enjoys replicating the costumes and settings down to the last detail.

A third style, Interpersonal, focuses on who will be impacted, who cares, who doesn't care and many other 'who' questions. They will make sure that each branch addresses people concerns in some way. Anthony always takes the discussion into the human arena. He wants to position each solution as an airtight response to actual people.

The Big Picture thinking style enjoys focusing on the overall vision that a mind map makes apparent and on the outcomes. Big Picture thinkers can see how the process moves forward toward a goal, and they can see the smaller picture at the same time. They will be sure the 'why' questions get covered. Miles has made his way in strategic thinking and the big picture is his baby. He loves Big Picture thinking and has trouble understanding people who want to constantly focus on details. Needless to say, Miles steers clear of G.Q. whenever possible.

A mind map can show present, past, and future all in one map. See below:

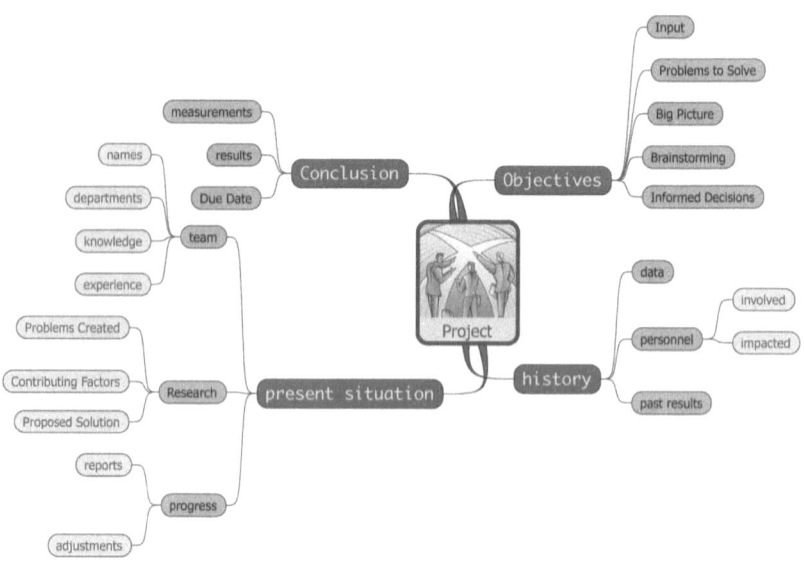

Developed using Novamind® Pro www.novamind.com

Here are five basic guidelines to follow when brainstorming:

1. Be sure you understand the question or problem. We'll talk about this in Chapter 7: Critical Thinking.
2. Brainstorm individually at times so that no one is influenced by what others say. Chapter 9: Individual Brainstorming goes into detail on how to do this.
3. Use one of the group brainstorming methods or tools for at least an hour or two, or until completion of the session.
4. Organize all the ideas; group or arrange all of them in some way that makes sense. A mind map or clustering ideas by topic are two good methods.
5. Important: Even at this point, hold off on any evaluation of ideas. You cluster them to see what's going on in your head or where the group seems to be heading. Your cluster might fit where you would like it to, or it may seem random but be on the lookout for where certain themes repeat, patterns are forming, or for additional ways to create connections between some of the ideas.

In the chapters that follow you will find many ways to help you brainstorm effectively and productively and especially to vary your methods, so it never gets boring.

Get out of your comfort zone and into your great ideas zone!

Use brainstorming for your problem solving because life may surprise you with more than one right answer.

We were taught in school that there is only one right answer – usually the one at the back of the book. In life and in business there is seldom only one right answer. We need to look at options, compare them, sometimes develop a pro and con list for the options, and then make a choice.

The purpose of brainstorming is to be able to choose between several good options vs. to find only one right answer. Instead use techniques that will cause you to come up with as many answers as possible, including some that are hilarious and some that could work better than others. Outrageous and interesting, unusual and out-of-the-box, crazy and "Hey, what if we could do that?" kinds of ideas, once explored as possibilities, often turn out to be great solutions.

All you need is a tool and a time limit.

How can you be more creative?

How can you do it every time you need to brainstorm?

If you need to get yourself or others motivated to work more creatively; if you need to come up with more innovative solutions to problems, then do this:

Pick out a brainstorming technique from this book and challenge the group to come up with 100 ideas before lunch. All you need is a tool and a time limit!

 STORM SESSION TWO

Despite the fact that his wardrobe choices were the butt of office, church and neighborhood jokes, G.Q. was actually quite fashion-conscious. He chose his sweater vests and lace-up short boots for specific reasons; reasons all his own. If ignorant fashion police wanted to assess his personal, style, so be it. G.Q. was never one to bother with popular opinion. Nevertheless, his keen awareness of clothing choices made him quite conscious of Amy Ann's rapid transformation.

Her ultra-mod style of "eco vamp," which consisted of a mixture of green army fabric and off-white linen mixed with slightly low-cut cotton shirts with short sleeves and tattoo type designs, seemed to transform overnight. The first thing that G.Q. noticed when he came in on Monday morning was her shoes. "The shoes always begin and end the statement." He had made that mental note to himself on many occasions. So, when he noticed that Amy Ann had traded her three and a half inch cork wedge shoes for a plain black half-inch sling back, he knew revolution was in the air – either that or civil war and she didn't seem the type for civil war. No, from his observations, Amy Ann was a general waiting for her troops to fall into formation.

On Tuesday, she had added a black eco-material purse that also resembled a book bag or even a briefcase. The ochre yellow leather knapsack decorated with suede patches and large buckles had disappeared.

Wednesday brought about a crisp blue-collared shirt with French cuffs, a gray A-lined skirt and…the softening of the pinkish red hair to a brownish auburn.

Finally, on Thursday, G.Q. noticed a sports watch with a stopwatch feature on Amy Ann's delicate wrist. She had a black notebook with sheets of information downloaded from the Internet neatly hole-punched and categorized.

G.Q. was also interested to note that the diamond nose stud had disappeared.

Miles also had not missed Amy Ann's purposeful approach to being a Facilitator, i.e., acting the part before she had officially obtained it. Instinctively he knew that his duty lay in giving her support and opportunities as far as it was within his power. On Friday, in fact, his boss, Arjun, mentioned to him that he needed a new approach to the Alaskan market. Advertising was not proving effective in Anchorage, Fairbanks, and Juneau. The market was reasonable, as these are the three most populous cities in Alaska, maybe as much as 1.5 million. Not a big market compared to LA, for instance, but still one worth a new approach.

Miles saw the possibilities and this time created a roster of participants, listing Amy Ann as the Facilitator. He presented the list to Arjun and asked him to approve another brainstorming session. He passed it up the chain of command casually, as a matter of protocol.

At their lunch on the Spiced Chai balcony that week, Miles had handed Amy Ann a slip of paper on which was written the URL for a Facilitator training organization web site. He had hired his 16-year-old dog-sitter to find it, and after two hours at 10 dollars an hour he'd come back with the URL. It seemed legitimate when Miles pulled it up, although he suspected that the whole thing was run from the front room of a pink ranch house in Pacifica, California.

Amy Ann couldn't have looked more grateful, and that was his reward.

The following Tuesday the group filed into the Double Mocha conference room. Amy Ann was already there, ready with sheets of paper for each person and a request that they all take off their shoes. She put on a CD of Abba and then after five minutes changed it to Procol Harum for another five minutes. Later she put on Bach and ended the session with Three Dog Night. Miles liked the experimentation, but Julia and G.Q. complained that the music made it too hard for them to concentrate. Anthony said that if half the group didn't like it, then it probably wasn't a good idea.

She took it like a pro, noting in her leather-bound blank book the effects of music. Not completely discouraged, she added, "I might just try a little deep Tibetan drumming another time."

The group had set aside three hours, and Amy Ann wrote in large letters across the wall, where she'd taped mammoth sheets of white paper, the question: "How can we penetrate the Anchorage and Juno markets more effectively?" Then she wrote down the methods of advertising currently being used and their effectiveness rates:

Newspaper	23 percent
Bus billboards	14 percent
Coupons	5 percent
TV	29 percent

The next question was: "What does the average (Alaskan) person see or use during a average day?"

Each member of the group had to contribute an idea in a rapid-fire round robin.

After 23 rounds, these results emerged:

Toothpaste tubes, doors, snow, microwave ovens, cereal boxes, clocks, radios, cell phones, credit cards, dogs and cats, children, windows, ice, fishermen, sleds, satellite dishes.

Amy Ann clustered these according to frequency:

1. Doors
2. Windows
3. snow

4. ice
5. cell phones
6. children
7. dogs and cats
8. microwave ovens
9. cereal boxes
10. toothpaste tubes
11. credit cards
12. radios
13. satellite dishes
14. sleds
15. fishermen

The group then took a brief break to write down ideas on their own. (This was when Amy Ann put on the Bach CD.)

Everyone stood up, and she led them in a series of six tai chi movements and deep breathing.

"Now," Amy Ann smiled mischievously, "I am going to assign each person in the room an identity and I want you to answer questions as that person, not as yourself. For instance, Julia, I'm going to say that you need to answer questions from now on the way that you think Miles would; Anthony, you need to answer questions the way that Julia would; G.Q., you're Anthony; and Anthony, you're Julia." Everyone looked rather shocked at having their personality thrown about so, but they took to the challenge quickly. "To make it easier," Amy Ann continued, I would like you each to move to the seat occupied by the person whom you've become. In other words, switch seats according to your assignment."

A period of musical chairs ensued during which Amy Ann played "In My Heart" by Three Dog Night.

"Doors?!" What can we do with doors?

Everyone started off slowly with this, since they were conscious of being in another character. Julia being Miles said, "We can create a song by The Doors, have it promote our products and pay establishments to attach a device to their doors that plays it every third time the door is opened."

Anthony, thinking like Julia, said, "We can give a free front door to the person who buys more than $1,000.00 worth of product in a six month period.

"That's not what I would say!" Julia snorted. "I'd say make little Cuckoo clocks with lots of doors that opened, and each one have a little coffee cup bird come out and sing a funny song."

"Sorry!" Anthony didn't seem the least perturbed by Julia's rebuff.

G.Q. posited, "I see a giant door hot air balloon floating in the sky above each city that blows up at 8:30 a.m. and showers everyone with coupon coins for a free cup of coffee for that day! Ha! That is so Anthony!"

Anthony smiled. "Yes, you got me."

Miles cleared his throat, "It's like this, every hardware store, every construction company, every door repair company will offer with each door a framed picture of a beautiful woman dressed in white gauze and surrounded by lilacs near an Artic ice field in spring. Her dress will be slightly transparent and her eyes closed enough to send shivers – blue eyes. The poster will simply say, "A cup of coffee shared means 40 years of friendship . . . NO! Make that a video on youtube.com and everywhere cyber. Yeah, that too, along with the poster."

Julia threw in, "The poster should come with a pound of coffee."

G.Q. offered, "How about a man sitting at a busy intersection on the median, at a nice table dressed up in a tux, with the woman in white sipping coffee from white china at morning rush hour, while a hot air balloon with the company's name floats overhead?"

Anthony, "In the winter – parkas"

Things went on in this manner for another hour until Amy Ann pushed the stop button on her sports watch.

Here are the new approaches that the group finally agreed to submit for the Alaska market:

1. Car dealerships installing a to-go coffee tumbler and a pound of coffee coupon in each new car door.
2. A coffee shop installed inside of the dealerships instead of the usual waiting room.
3. Upholstered furniture retailers, giving away a coupon for 10 free cups of coffee to each person who purchases a soft, comfy chair or couch.
4. Each preschool in the area posting a company ad on their front doors.

5. Combining a TV commercial for diapers with a promise of child-friendly "chill time" at participating stores and then providing a play area with videos, crayons and a play-partner attendant. Also closed-caption cartoons on Saturday morning.
6. Each store hosting a snowman contest with a special on hot chocolate with marshmallows.
7. Each store offering a "kids' tea" once a week with Alice in Wonderland and/or the Mad Hatter attending.
8. Each store hosting a "singles night" one night a week, where the center floor is cleared for dancing. (G.Q. said the dancing would never work, and Amy Ann had to remind him not to censor even at the end.)
9. Ads on the backs of kids' breakfast cereal boxes.
10. A "coffee truck" that comes through neighborhoods early every morning.

Arjun and the Alaska marketing team were quite pleased with the team's results and decided to call upon them on a more regular basis.

YOUR PERFECT STORM

Here is a problem for which you can create solutions. Please create four groups of solutions according to the four thinking styles: Rational, Organized, Big Picture and Interpersonal.

Problem:

Farid owns a fleet of cabs. He is suffering a loss of revenue because his drivers keep going back to their home countries to visit their families for months at a time. He can't keep the whole fleet of 100 cars all operated by American-born drivers. Besides, he likes his international drivers. What incentive or contractual stipulation can Farid use to keep his drivers operating for at least nine months a year?

A – Rational solutions

B – Detailed, organized solutions

C – Big Picture solutions

D – Interpersonal solutions

Chapter 6

15 Non-Rules for Brainstorming

"There are no rules here - we're trying to accomplish something."

THOMAS A. EDISON

Monkey Business
by Will Bullas, with permission of the artist. www.willbullas.com

The main rule of thumb for being a good brainstormer is not to feel any inhibitions. Speak up. Go for it! Let ideas be crazy, silly, and inconsistent. Break all the rules about how to think about business and just whirl around the world with your imagination in high gear, no holds barred.

To help you slip into this free-thinking rocket ship, here are a few brainstorming non-rules (meant to free you not to tie you down):

1. Brainstorm only the questions first to frame it appropriately.

   Note: How do you usually approach problem solving? Are you quick to come up with a solution and then move on? There is a much better way:

   Get all those questions out on paper before even thinking of solutions.

   Before attempting to brainstorm solutions, take as much time as possible to brainstorm only the *questions* to ask.

   Use these seven questions: Who?, What?, When?, Why?, Why not?, How?, How much?

2. Brainstorm silently or alone beforehand, even if you are going to be brainstorming in a group, so you know and remember what was going on in your own head and what your own thoughts were.

   Once someone hears someone else's ideas, it starts a whole new train of thought and his (or her) own ideas that were in his head a moment ago will be forgotten.

3. When you are brainstorming out loud in a group, make quick notes of any ideas that pop into your head so that you can keep on listening without losing those thoughts.

4. **Write it down, right away!** Be sure all ideas are recorded so that the complete list and emerging patterns can be reworked and developed further. Even ideas about which someone says 'we tried that before and it didn't work,' need to be scrutinized again. After all, there must be a shred of something important there, or it wouldn't keep coming up. It needs to be viewed from some new angles.

5. Use knowledge and research two ways. First, have resources available to answer questions, at least about your main topic. Second, don't let the most knowledgeable person dominate the session. The person with the least knowledge may have a fresh viewpoint that leads to extremely productive ideas. Your facilitator must be comfortable asking

dominant personality people to back down and allow time for others to speak.

6. Be sure the group is passionate about the subject. *You might need to talk about the value of ideas.* Who would get excited about racking their brain for new ideas unless the subject really interests them? Not everyone shows their passion by jumping up and down and yelling out ideas, but the energy of passion about a subject will come out in many different ways.

7. Be absolutely clear on the goal. What problem are you trying to solve? In what direction are you trying to take the company? What new products would customers love? What issues within the company need fresh approaches? Be sure everyone understands and agrees on the goal, and that there is agreement on the definition of the words and concepts. If not, the group members will be taking different directions and won't seem to be working together.

8. Have a diverse group. Diversity for the sake of variety and quantity of ideas is based on a number of categories. You especially need diversity of thinking styles.

9. Once you start brainstorming out loud be sure to pay attention -- to listen to what everyone is saying. Ask for clarification, if necessary, but make no judgments. This means not even saying, "That is a good idea." Every idea is a good one as you are gathering them all and getting everything written down.

   If someone is praised for their idea, all the others will subconsciously feel that they need to go in that direction, and abandon the direction their thoughts were taking. Though it sounds like a compliment and a good thing to do to encourage, it actually can be a damper on idea generation.

10. Encourage everyone's wholehearted participation and *listen for details and examples* that might trigger more ideas for you and others.

11. Use different methods; vary the technique; vary the person facilitating if you are not using a professional facilitator; vary your process often if you meet fairly regularly to brainstorm. Even during a brainstorming session, if it is to last more than a couple of hours, you might take a break and then pick one path you were developing and use another method. You need to work the method and subject long enough to

be fruitful. Don't give up too soon. Also don't drag out a session and method so long that everyone feels bored, which leads to the next tip.

12. Stay with each method long enough to allow the ideas to come to the surface and develop. Even wait out some bumps in the road and silence in the room.

13. Use a scribe whose only job is to capture every idea. For a particularly large and important brainstorming subject you might consider hiring a specialist who does this well. Put butcher paper or any large sheets of blank paper up on most of the walls so anyone can add to the notes. Or if you have and use white boards around the room, then capture the boards with a photo or by someone who transcribes it exactly as drawn. If you used individual sheets, collect all the sheets and have all the ideas put into a database. This will allow the facilitator to concentrate on keeping the process moving and not have to worry about getting it all transcribed.

14. What to do with those long lists of ideas? You have a number of choices that depend on time available and what needs to be done with the first big brainstorming effort. One person can organize the list into natural clusters. The largest clusters may be an indication of the relevance or importance of that set of ideas. Or, you can have the group figure out how they would cluster the ideas. This usually starts more brainstorming, generating additional ideas, which is great. If the clusters of ideas are large enough, assign each cluster to a small team to develop further.

 ### STORM SESSION 3

"You know," Anthony said, as he fell into step next to Julia, "I think the powers that be are starting to wake up to our little brainstorming group." He smiled conspiratorially, "In fact, I would put money on the possibility that we are becoming something of an item."

Julia smiled, "You don't say. Well, I'm glad to hear it. This company needs some shaking up if it's going to keep its market share. Why not harvest the creative thinking of its best people?"

Anthony laughed, "Yes, of course, its best people!" He narrowed his eyes as they came to a stop in front of Julia's office door. "You know what I'd like a shot at?"

"What?"

"I'd like a shot at brand renewal to counteract all that bad press about the hormones and the rain forest."

"Our Achilles heel, our wound."

"Yes. Why not get 'The People' in on a brilliant defensive maneuver?"

Julia walked into her glass-walled office, leaving the door open. "Actually, I think Miles mentioned that we have something scheduled next week." She checked for e-mail from Amy Ann. It looks like she's now scheduling the sessions. "I hope there's no more music."

"I don't mind music if there's dancing too," Anthony showed off his disco moves.

Julia laughed, "Ahh Anthony, if only my husband had your joie de vivre! I'm afraid his idea of dancing is when he stands up and almost topples over. Oh look here, Amy Ann has written that we are each required to spend 30 minutes brainstorming on our own. She's written up a procedure . . . hmm."

Anthony turned to leave, "What's the question?"

"Oh, it's different this time. The question is, 'How can a new store on an exclusive resort island compete with the beloved general store where all the residents hang out – and several are in their 70's and 80's?"

"Why do they want to break into such a risky market? Why not just add a nickel to airport prices and be done with it? Does someone up there need to feel pain?" Anthony shook his head in disbelief and compassion for the local store owners.

Julia shooed him out of her office. "We'll get to have our say someday, for now this is good practice, don't you think?"

Anthony gave her a long searching look. "You've got something up your sleeve. I can tell. Julia, you minx! What sort of trouble are you cooking up?"

"Out, out!" Julia gave him only the sternest smile and then turned to the pile of papers on her desk.

(10 days later)

Amy Ann surveyed the group with a sense of authority and pride that fit her like a glove.

"Did you all do your individual brainstorming for 30 minutes?" Miles waved his paper in the air gaily and said nothing. "Please pass your list of ideas to me and I will make a cluster. You all know what the question is," Amy Ann pointed to the question written in large letters on the board.

"I'm going to pass out these two pieces of paper. Each one is divided into 10 squares on the front and 10 on the back. You have one minute to write an idea down in the square and pass it to the next person. Do this 40 times."

Miles raised his hand.

"Yes, Miles?'

"Miss Facilitator, how come we have to do it so many times? I can't think of 40 ideas."

"Actually, Miles, you can. The more you have to press yourself to come up with something, the better the ideas become. In fact," she pulled out another page with squares drawn on it, "let's make it 60 times." The group groaned in disbelief.

"I know for a fact that my brain cannot sustain such stress, such over-exertion. I'm sure of it!" Anthony exclaimed.

Amy Ann smiled and sat down in an accommodating gesture. "I tell you what. Just give it a try and see what happens. If it's a total failure, then we won't do it again. We'll play cards or something else, but none of us really knows what we're capable of under great pressure do we?"

Miles stood up and stuck out his chest. "Ready to march, General!"

Amy Ann took off her watch and held it in front of her. "Good. Remember, no matter how farfetched, how silly or weird your idea is, you must write it down. And, no commenting on what anyone else has written."

"Everyone please stand, take three deep breaths, move your arms in wide circles and then sit down." The group did as they were told, and then Amy Ann pushed the green button on her watch and shouted, "Go!"

The sound of paper sliding across the table and the scratching of pens were the only cracks in the silence of the room. Like a tightly wound clock, the paper moved rapidly from hand to hand. When it began to slow down, Amy Ann called out, "Get it moving people!"

At one point G.Q. passed a giant handkerchief across his brow. Giggling erupted from time to time. Finally, after 55 minutes, Amy Ann called, "Stop!"

The group fell back in their chairs and Anthony rushed out to the men's' room. Julia pulled a bottle of blueberry juice out of her purse. "Brain food!" she announced to no one in particular.

Here is the cluster that Amy Ann compiled for The Question: 'How can a new store on an exclusive resort island compete with the beloved general store where all the residents hang out – median age 70?"

Products	Events	Setting
A birthday cake for each resident (150 total) on their birthday. Free to birthday person.	A giant group cross-word puzzle. A movie screen at night showing silent films from the 30's	A big huge porch with rocking chairs.
Non-gluten pastries with agave instead of sugar.	A message board where people leave anonymous messages for each other and another board where the funniest are posted.	Exposed rafters.
Soup	board games, including "strip poker" night – down to shirt and pants.	A fireplace.
Coffees from different countries, like Vietnamese, Russian etc.	Group novel, written one page per person in an "coffee table-sized" book.	Crow's nest on the roof.
"Pillow packets" of fresh coffee smell and fresh baked cookie smell. (especially good for those trying to sell their properties.)		Steel drum set
Neck massage		Bicycle peddles attached to some tables.
Foot massage		Flat screen TV showing constant satellite weather
Medicinal teas		
Scalp massage		
Coffee brewed in a percolator over a flame		
Hot toddies		
Corn products: Popcorn, cornbread, grits, corn on the cob		

YOUR PERFECT STORM

1. Pick something you and a friend have discussed before. Spend 30 minutes coming up with 30 ideas with the friend.
2. Leave one another and meet again in 15 minutes. Write down five new ideas each.

3. Do not talk to anyone during the 15 minutes apart.
4. Cluster your results based on any categories the two of you notice.
5. Create a final mind map
6. Write down your ultimate choices.

CHAPTER 7

CRITICAL THINKING: THE WHO?, WHAT?, HOW? QUESTIONS

"To raise new questions, new possibilities, to regard old problems from a new angle, requires creative imagination and marks real advance in science."

ALBERT EINSTEIN

"Does a Bear Think in the Woods?"
by Will Bullas, with permission of the artist. www.willbullas.com

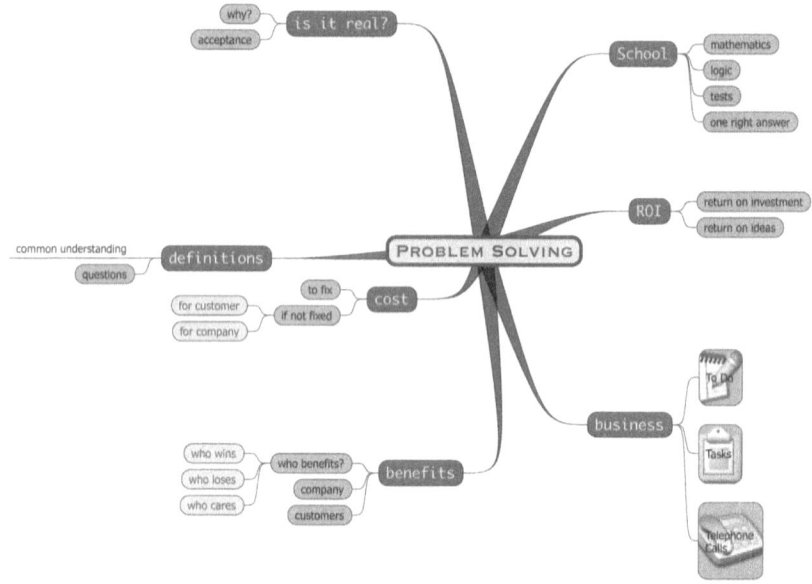

Problem solving

Business problems crop up every day. When we were in school we were taught that a problem has one answer and it is our job to figure out that one answer. But business life, and life in general, is not like that. Most of the time there are multiple possible answers and there could be many good answers.

> *"Our doubts are traitors,*
> *And make us lose the good we oft might win*
> *By fearing to attempt."*
> ~ William Shakespeare (1564 - 1616),
> Measure for Measure, *"Act 1 scene 4"*

It is too easy, too comfortable, and usually a mistake to think that you are searching for the one right answer. Instead in business brainstorming we are looking for as many options as possible to be considered and then make a choice or choices among them. If we think there is only one right answer we will jump on the first answer that comes up that would work. Usually the first idea is one that comes up fast because it is common and over-used. Even if it does turn out to be the best answer once you have considered other alternatives, you will know why. You will make your choice because it won the comparison discussion, not just because it was the first and only idea expressed.

Business Problem to Brainstorming Solutions

The first part of business brainstorming is making sure that everyone agrees that there is a problem and how to define it. The problem should be written in the form of a question that all participants in the discussion agree.

Business brainstorming the problem means spending time listing as many solution options as possible before doing any analysis. During the brainstorming of options it is important to apply the usual rules of listing everything without any value judgments or comments. It doesn't help at this point to know that someone tried one of those options before and it didn't work. The larger the number of options listed the more likely that a few, or some combinations, would rise to the top to be considered further. Often a seemingly crazy idea turns out to be the one that with a bit of changes wins out in the end.

Problem Finding

Not too many people in business would think looking for problems makes any sense. Don't we all have enough of them to deal with without looking for more? Yet if you and your business associates can brainstorm to discover what problems customers are likely to find, and you can find them first so they can be fixed, how might that help your business? Clustering may be a good tool for this purpose. It is the most open-ended, free form, receptive process that allows simply spilling out and writing everything down without regard to appropriateness – to begin with. You can be expansive, even have fun in the process.

Problem solving for businesses is different.

To do it well, it requires several steps:

1. Understand the problem.
2. Make sure that solving it is worth more than the cost of solving it.
3. Brainstorm and explore options and alternatives.
4. Choose one or more of the options.
5. Implement.
6. Monitor and make changes if the solution is not working out.

We've been scratching the surface of brainstorming so far. While we've learned how to generate ideas quickly and capture them, there is much more to brainstorming than churning out creative ideas. At its best, brainstorming actually establishes solid foundations of reason and achievement. Our group working for the large coffee shop franchise operation has already begun to wonder why they should come up with the ideas assigned to them as opposed to other ideas.

The next and most important lesson on brainstorming is learning how to devise the initial question(s). The methods discussed in this chapter help individuals to clarify and understand the central problem and then think more deeply and critically about it before making decisions.

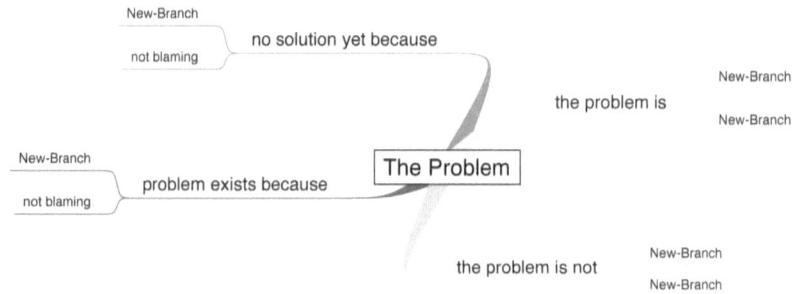

Critical thinking is best done with someone with whom you have developed mutual trust. If it's a team of people who haven't ever met before, pay attention during the first few sessions. If you see that one or more members are unable to participate fully because they cannot trust the others, then replace them.

Yes, you can challenge yourself and search for deeper understanding on your own through reading and analyzing what you read and by finding quiet time to just think. But for most of us, having a buddy or a team to think through and challenge each other will result in more information being brought into the discussion and better decisions in the long run. Brainstorming for critical thinking is more spontaneous and prolific in a group.

> *"The important thing is not to stop questioning."*
> ~ Albert Einstein 1879-1955

How to Uncover the Real Question(s)

1. Understand the problem. This is not trivial. More often than not, the first attempt at stating a problem just gets at the surface of the issue. It might only describe the symptoms and not the core problem.

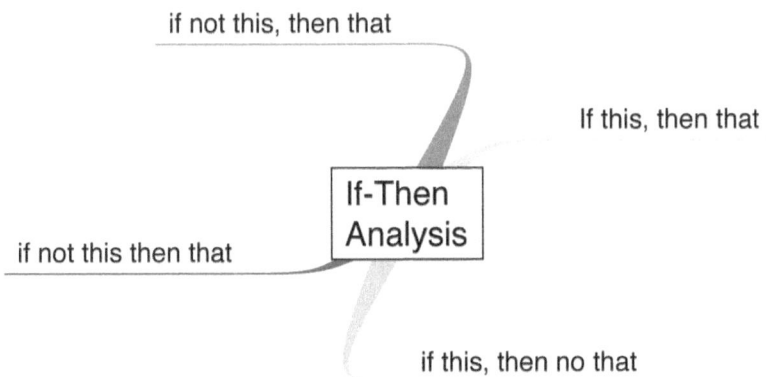

2. Brainstorm all the questions that would help you understand the problem better. During this stage of a brainstorm session only questions are suggested and listed. If someone tries to move towards a solution, suggest that they hold that thought until everyone is sure what issue they are trying to understand better.

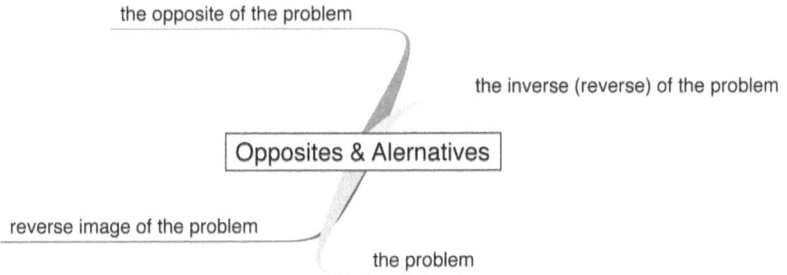

When brainstorming critical thinking issues, it is more important to cover the topic completely than when you are doing freewheeling idea generation. List categories of questions and work on each category in turn.

Step 1: Ask:
- Who?
- What?
- Why?
- Why not?
- When?
- Where?
- How?
- How much?
- Who cares?
- Who doesn't care?

These categories usually bring out most of the necessary questions. Remember to focus only on the questions that need answers during this stage of brainstorming. Below you can see a mind map of the question generating process.

Limiting this stage of critical thinking allows you to get all the questions out and think more about the problem before starting to think about the solutions. Your later thinking about options for solutions will be richer and more creative if you go through this stage first.

 ## STORM SESSION 4

Amy Ann had been gone for three days, attending the Facilitator-training workshop, which turned out to be in Chicago. Miles had cleared the way for corporate funding of the training and had spoken more than once to Arjun and Theo about the need for a full-time Facilitator in the company. They had agreed in concept, but wanted to address various types and levels of problems before committing to brainstorming as an integral part of doing business.

Finally, Amy Ann returned just in time for Miles to spring a new assignment on her.

She studied the memo he handed her for several minutes. "Do you have any questions?" he asked her.

She raised her dark brown eyes to his and slowly smiled. "Is that supposed to be a double-entendre? I can see that the assignment is to come up with the actual questions, so, no I don't have any questions about the assignment . . . And," she added, "I don't, as yet, have any questions on the topic either."

"Touché!" Miles couldn't help but feel that in scolding him, she was flirting with him just a little bit. "I'll leave the arrangements to you, then." He snapped his fingers and walked away whistling "The Way You Look Tonight."

When the big day for the question brainstorming session rolled around, G.Q. stationed himself near the front desk to evaluate Amy Ann's choice of uniform. (He referred to all outfits as uniforms.)

She entered unassumingly in a muted lime green shirtdress, a wide black belt and the same sling backs he had noticed earlier. Walking by casually, he commented, "Nice dress, Amy Ann."

"Thank you," she smiled openly at him, clearly confident in her manner this Thursday morning.

Julia also commented on Amy Ann's dress, "Green on Thursday, Amy Ann, good for you!"

"What do you mean?" The younger woman looked puzzled.

"Green is the color of the heart chakra, it stands for relationship, and Thursday is the day of the week that corresponds to the heart chakra."

Amy Ann raised her eyebrows. "I see. The heart chakra. Interesting."

G.Q. looked slightly annoyed, as was his habit whenever Julia started her mumbo jumbo talk.

Anthony said nothing, drinking in the information, his mind preoccupied with endless inner equations.

After they had all assembled, this time in the Blueberry Crumb Muffin training room, which had a glass wall overlooking the city, Miles stood up. "Before we get started Amy Ann, I would like to say a few words." Miles looked out over the vast urban skyline, "I think it's important, as we contemplate ever deeper issues, to remind ourselves of our vision: a vision keeps passion alive. The vision I have is of this company unfolding and expanding into all of the nooks and crannies of the world until our name comes to mean unity, oneness

– literally "a meeting place." That's my vision and what keeps me going." His voice wavered as he sat down. "I invite you all to share it."

No one spoke for a couple of minutes.

"Thank you, Miles," Amy Ann acknowledged him gracefully. "Does anyone wish to respond or address Miles' comments?"

G.Q. spoke up, "I don't want to sound like a stick-in-the-mud, but to be exact, Miles did say that that was *his* vision. I know he's invited us to share it, but I personally have my own vision, which does not include colonizing the far corners of the Earth. I am not on a crusade, an evangelical exposition or quest for dominance under the guise of One Love."

"Are you insane?" Miles bolted out of his chair, his face livid. "You're twisting my words!"

"I hate fighting," Anthony spoke up. "Although I know that conflict is the engine of all relationships, it really is upsetting."

"Perhaps," Amy Ann moved to stand between G.Q. and Miles, "You are right, Anthony. This is a perfect opportunity for us all to look at how different thinking styles can influence our perspectives." She turned to G.Q., "G.Q. what is your vision? We know what it isn't. Can you tell us what it *is*?"

G.Q. sat quietly looking down at the carpet, "I think," he began carefully, "That my vision is well-oiled flexibility. I honestly don't care if the company sells coffee around the world in posh parlor-like settings or if it drops bags of insect and worm entrails over Third World nations. I just want it to be able to bend and adapt to the market and customer needs, so that it remains fluid and viable. For me the big picture is in the detailed inner workings and decisions of the company on a day-to-day basis."

"I get it!" Julia said, "You're interested in long-term viability – the vital signs, blood pressure, breathing and all that. Miles is celebrating what's going on now with a great expectation of success."

"Do you both see how your different thinking styles, Miles being Big Picture and G.Q. being Organized contributes to your perspectives?" Amy Ann prodded.

"Yes, I see that," Miles acknowledged.

"I'm sorry if I offended you," G.Q. got up and offered Miles his hand. Miles shook it and grinned.

"I need an aged burgundy right now!" Anthony breathed a sigh of relief.

Amy Ann opened a cooler and began putting various beverages on the table. She then pulled out a box of muffins, scones, cookies and chips. Everyone happily munched down, and relaxed in their chairs.

CRITICAL THINKING: THE WHO?, WHAT?, HOW QUESTIONS • 75

Pulling down a projector screen, Amy Ann began a PowerPoint presentation. "Here's the situation, people, for which we have been asked to generate one or more questions. As you can see, this issue does not have to do with product or store placement. We have significant franchise defaulting that has begun to occur since last April." She clicked to another slide. "Also, you can see that those franchises that do not default are not fully compliant with contractual guidelines, thereby corrupting the brand. In short, we have a sort of slow mutiny on our hands."

She turned on the lights.

"I have to say that I didn't know about this, but I'm not surprised either," Julia said.

"Right." Amy Ann returned to the front of the room. "I'd like to remind all of you that we can come up with any questions that we want, without judgment of ourselves or others. There are no wrong responses, and there is always a multitude of possible answers."

"The first thing we can do, is work through this list of who?, what?, why? questions. When we've finished, I think we will be in a better position to formulate the final questions to ask," she concluded.

- Who?
- What?
- Why?
- Why not?
- When?
- Where?
- How?
- How much?
- Who cares?
- Who doesn't care?

"Do we have to go in that order?" Anthony asked.

"No, not at all, but we have to go fast, so let's start somewhere in the middle, how about *How*?" Everyone gave his or her approval.

"We'll start with Julia and go clockwise around the room, moving rapidly. I'll write down everything you say."

"How are we vetting franchise buyers before they purchase?" Julia asked.

"How do we communicate our expectations?" Miles threw in.

"How do we decide that they're not in compliance?" G.Q.

"How does the franchisee perceive the company?" Anthony asked.

"How do we know that the franchisees are hurting the brand?" – Julia

"How can a customer tell the differenced between a compliant and a non-compliant store?" – Miles

"How does a franchise get classified as successful and profitable?" – G.Q. "In other words, whose standard is it and who applies it?"

"How can the company investigate these instances to determine if they're even related?" – Anthony.

After 30 minutes, Amy Ann put up her hand and said, "Next question: Why? Go!"

"Why is this the first time the company is concerned about defaults?" – Julia

"Why do the franchisees not ask for help before defaulting?" – Miles

"Why did we not anticipate these issues?" – G.Q.

"Why are the legal and financial aspects the only indicators of failure?" – Anthony

After 30 minutes on the question, "Why?", Amy Ann dimmed the lights, played Tibetan drumming music and encouraged people to lay down on the floor. Miles did lay down an arm's length from Amy Ann. Julia stood up and did slow circular stretches, G.Q. went out for a cigarette and Anthony stood looking out the window with his fingers on the glass.

The group continued for another hour and a half. At the end of the brainstorming session, they had a number of possible questions, but more importantly, a feeling of trust seemed to have solidified between them. They were becoming a real team.

YOUR PERFECT STORM

Here is a situation:

You run a computer manufacturing plant in Ireland. Most of the product is sold in the United States. With new trade tariffs levied by the European Union, profit margins have been cut to the degree that they almost match the positive incentives initially provided by Ireland to establish the plant there. Now that the plant is well established, closing it down would entail even greater losses. The computers manufactured in this plant are large processing units normally sold to other manufacturing companies for the maintenance of large databases. Schools and universities also purchase these units. Make any assumptions you need for information not specified or describe a situation of your own that is similar.

Using the 10 "who?, what?, how?" questions provided in this chapter, work with at least two other people to create five core questions that can lead brainstormers to solutions.

Write your final questions here:

1.

2.

3.

4.

5.

CHAPTER 8

EVALUATING CRITICAL THINKING QUESTIONS AND GENERATING NEW SOLUTIONS

Critical thinking is about understanding with as much depth as possible. It is not about being critical or negative about anything.

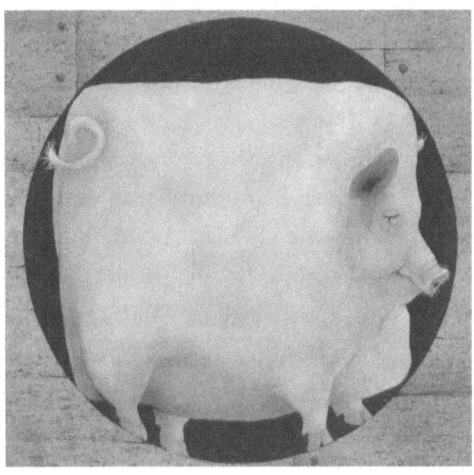

A Square Pig in the Round Hole,
by Will Bullas, with permission of the artist. www.willbullas.com

In the last chapter, you worked to take a situation apart and explore all of the different ways of thinking about it. The goal was to generate core questions that addressed the real issues and then allowed you to brainstorm realistic solutions.

In this chapter, we'll discover how to take on these big questions without feeling bogged down so that your creative energy can keep going. We want to push through what we perceive as obstacles to the very best ideas. At the same time, of course, we have to accept certain concrete limitations, such as budget, location and rules of law.

The brainstorming of critical thinking questions accomplishes:
- Better and longer lists of options/possibilities
- Better analysis of options without falling into analysis paralysis
- Better buy-in from the group which had the opportunity to be part of the critical thinking process.

The following procedure is both simple and complex. It is simple because anyone can do it if they apply disciplined focus. It is complex because it requires disciplined focus and freewheeling, passionate, fun-loving, creative energy. What about you? Can you do it?

1. Get the questions answered that are necessary before working on the central problem. Some questions are about information or facts and someone just needs to look those up. Some questions require an opinion - yours, someone in the room, or possibly someone else. If it is someone else, go and ask.

2. Once the questions are answered and the problem is clearly understood, it is time to brainstorm options for solutions. This brainstorming session should allow time for many possibilities to surface. Here are solution questions that allow for all possible options to be explored:
   - If anything were possible, what would we do?
   - If we could get all the funds needed, what would we do?
   - If we had enough resources, what would we do?
   - What else?

3. Now add a touch of reality without making it feel like cold water being thrown on the group. OK, so we don't have unlimited funds and resources.
   - How could we still accomplish that objective?
   - Which of the options listed are possible?

- Which ones can we do enough to make a difference?

4. Pick a few options and run them through a pro-and-con list. Everything has some pros and some cons. Everything you do has "side effects." The question can be: Which options have pros outweighing cons?

 STORM SESSION 5

"In the last brainstorming session, we created the following questions, which I've mind mapped and handed out to each of you." Amy Ann pointed to the mind map that was also represented on a large display board at the front of the room."

The group looked at Amy Ann's mind map and reflected, but without enthusiasm.

"To tell you the truth," Madam Facilitator, "I know it's our job and all, but I'm feeling quite beat at the moment," Anthony confessed.

"Yes," Julia agreed, "I'm in a bit of the doldrums too. I don't feel very enthusiastic about asking these questions."

Amy Ann fingered the long strand of jade hanging around her neck. "What about you two, Miles and G.Q.? Are you out of it too?"

Miles put his head down on the table and feigned sleep. G.Q. shrugged. "I'd rather be playing chess in an open field with human pieces authentically dressed, if you want to know the truth."

"I see..." Amy Ann paused, clearly caught up in her own unexpected brainstorming session.

At that moment, the door to the Chocolate Schnapps room opened and three people walked in. Amy Ann recognized Miles' boss, Arjun, and she guessed that the Jimi Hendrix fellow was Theo, the famous Gen X, out-of-the-box VP in charge of franchise account maintenance. The third individual, she did not recognize. Her small mousy face was framed by giant glasses, and her body swam in a too-big black suit; the woman accompanying the men wore no make-up, flats and, from what Amy Ann could see, had not even the barest glimmer of jewelry anywhere on her body. Her hands, ear lobes, neck, and wrists were all bare of baubles. Amy Ann became acutely aware of her triple looped strand of jade and gold beads and the various bracelets and earrings adorning her body.

All the men in the room had stood up respectfully and the only person seated was Julia.

"Let us introduce ourselves," Arjun stepped forward and shook Amy Ann's hand. "My name is Arjun Bux; this is Theo Wilson and this is Madeline Gegoux. I work with Miles on the Western division communication strategies, Theo is my supervisor and Madeline is our CFO. We're quite lucky to have her today. We're just going to sit in and watch if that's OK with you?"

"Nice to meet you all." Amy Ann realized that her "day" had come. Clearly, her dreams of promotion to full-time Facilitator would either be stunningly fulfilled or dashed according to the session's unfolding. "Of course, have a seat. I have to warn you that brainstorming is very different from finding the one right answer. We all have open minds and aren't afraid to contribute anything that comes to us. We don't censor and judge."

She looked around at her assembled crew who had just minutes before staged a minor mutiny.

No, she couldn't count on them to come through just for her; they would have to be genuinely inspired.

"You're just in time. Our group has a case of low energy level and I am moving the meeting into the lab." She picked up her clipboard and the poster with the mind map illustrated on it. "If you would all follow me to the fourth floor." Amy Ann moved forward, G.Q. thought like Ulysses S. Grant fording a tributary before setting up camp.

Luckily, the lab, a replica of a coffee shop interior, was in good order with tables, chairs, sofas and sales counter all clean and orderly. The case had been recently filled and the machines stood shiny and ready to spew out black elixir or churn smoothies the colors of the rainbow.

Everyone sat down in different chairs and Madeline raised her hand. "Amy Ann, would it disrupt your process if the three of us participated? I think we would learn more that way than by simply watching."

"That is a great idea!" Amy Ann handed each person the following list:
- If anything were possible, what would we do?
- If we could get all the funds needed, what would we do?
- What else?

"Today, I thought we would evaluate one question from each category for 15 to 20 minutes each. The key to success is to move quickly from one person to another and to remain non-judgmental about any contribution." Arjun, Theo and Madeline nodded.

"To start off, I have some information here about the financial issues facing our franchisees, a typical operating budget, a loan structure, a pie chart showing net vs. gross, and a time map showing what a typical owner does during a seven-day period. This list," she continued as she pulled out several pages stapled together, "shows the types of marketing initiatives that our competitors have taken in the last two years and charts their success rate."

As everyone pored over his or her information, Amy Ann felt a great upwelling of gratitude in her heart for Julia. It was Julia who had suggested that she prepare the detailed statistics and make extra copies. She must have known about the "visit" and wanted Amy Ann to be prepared.

While the group was reading, Amy Ann set out a plate of brownies and a thermos of coffee.

After 10 minutes the group agreed to start. The first question they chose to focus on was:

"What incentives can we offer to franchises to keep them invested during inevitable down times?"

Amy Ann grabbed her marker, opened to a clean page on the display tablet and pushed the green button on her watch. "Start with Miles, going clockwise. Go!"

"Flexible pay structures."

"High, medium and low operational plans with the ability to switch back and forth."

"Franchise clusters, where two to five all work together as a consortium."

Theo interjected, "I believe that would violate our existing by-laws."

Amy Ann smiled. Thank you, Theo. It may be disconcerting at first to hear ideas thrown out that you don't think are appropriate, but the point of a brainstorming session is to dig deep and pull out as many ideas as possible. To do that we have to refrain from censoring or commenting."

Theo laughed, "I got it!"

Amy Ann, pointed at him, "Your turn."

"OK, 50percent off all wholesale product for the first year, then decreasing the discount on a staggered basis for five years."

"Web and magazine advertising for free for one year."

"Financial consultants on-call for personal visits at no cost."

"Child care vouchers."

"Mental health retreats twice a year at wholesale prices: featuring the Cayman Islands and Bermuda."

"Shares in a profitable dairy farm."

"Four acres of coffee plants."

"Celebrity visits every quarter - like country music stars for some and positive thinking gurus and soap opera stars."

"Belly dancing lessons."

"Partnering with pottery makers."

"Allowing them to set up booths at sporting events."

"Partnering with crafts and plant vendors to have small markets outside their entrances where possible."

"Bicycle drive-throughs."

"Shoot a YouTube soap opera in a different store each week, and get locals to act in it."

"Coupon promotion in the office supply stores."

"Provide a funeral package for franchise owners to market to funeral parlors as a catered or onsite wake."

"Coin operated merry-go-rounds and buckin' broncos in the front for kids."

Partner with Laundromats – the new eco kind.

Sunday morning coffee, juice, pastries and the paper delivered to your door by our company franchise - for a premium.

After two hours, the group had a list of possible solutions in each category.

The management team said their goodbyes and left laughing and talking among themselves excitedly.

"Team," Amy Ann addressed them all, "thanks for rallying. You did a great job!"

Anthony let out a whoop! And on that note the group dispersed quickly, in a somewhat self-congratulatory mood.

"Thank you, Julia."

"You're welcome, Amy Ann. I'm glad to see this brainstorming becoming more integrated in to our decision-making processes."

YOUR PERFECT STORM

Cluster and then mind map the questions you came up with from the last exercise.

Pick one question and go around asking it for thirty minutes with four to five people participating one at a time, or as few as two, by phoning them or stopping by their office.

Write your six best result solutions down here:

1.

2.

3.

4.

5.

6.

Chapter 9

Individual Brainstorming

Learning to be more "whole brained[1]" in thinking on our own allows us to view the subject from the four most common perspectives.

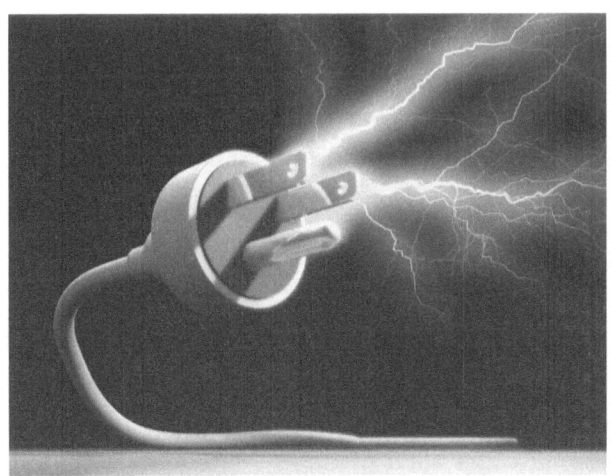

© ktsdesign - Fotolia.com

We've touched on individual brainstorming several times in the preceding chapters. Clearly, it helps for each person to spend some time thinking in different modes and coming up with ideas before they join a group brainstorming session.

Three primary benefits exist for individual brainstorming. They are:

1. Learning how to think in different modes : Rational, Organized, Interpersonal and Big Picture.
2. Accessing brainstorming ideas when you are the only person available.
3. Stimulating the group session with individually generated ideas.

Ways to Enter Into A Different Mindset

When you are brainstorming on your own, follow this procedure for the best results:

A. Write your question down and put it on a piece of paper or a board, or type it on your computer screen in big letters.

B. Start with your personal mode of thinking and brainstorm 50 ideas in two minutes. (No cheating.)

C. Now, move to a new page and under the question type one of these statements:

- When I think of the bottom line on this issue, I think of:
- The most important details to consider are:
- In relation to the other issues and components, this problem is:
- This is how it fits into our/my vision or big picture plans:
- This is exciting and innovative because:
- The main people affected by this issue are:
- This is how the people would be affected with this solution:

Take another stab at generating ideas for the problem, but this time focus on one of the perspectives represented above. In other words, if you are a rational thinker come up with 50 solutions in two minutes that address the problem from one of the alternative styles, such as an organizational detail-oriented perspective.

For example, if the question is, "How can I get people to stay at my presentations longer?"

A Big Picture answer might be: Make the material more exciting with stories and pictures.

An Organized answer might be: Don't give them credit unless they stay to the end. Have people sign in and out.

A Rational answer might be: Split the material up into three sections and ask more questions of the audience.

An Interpersonal answer might be: Put cushions on the seats, offer free drinks and snacks and give away a series of prizes at the end.

Create four pages, one for each style of thinking and use up eight minutes generating your ideas. You can type them or write them longhand.

If you've been brainstorming alone, it's always good to cluster your ideas and show them to someone else to get their feedback. If you really do not have anyone else to work with, I suggest putting the ideas aside for a couple of days and then looking at them fresh. This is almost like having another pair of eyes.

Sometimes, you may not have the luxury of waiting two days but must proceed to evaluate your ideas (as to which are the promising). This is why it is so essential that you practice the self-discipline to rapidly create many solutions in a very short period of time. This is the only way to force your brain to give up its riches without another person present to spur you on.

If possible have one or more tools or methods to jump-start your thinking. Tools with questions posed, such as the KnowBrainer® Whackpack®, and Thinkpak® can be used individually - as well as in groups. [See the list of resources at the back of this book for where to purchase these items.]

Starting Individually and then moving to a group: "Piggybacking"

Piggybacking is simply taking ideas generated individually to a group and spending the group brainstorming session expanding on those ideas. Great ideas often come from expanding on an idea that might have been discarded. No negativity and no value judgments, even positive ones, at this point. Brain writing or challenging everyone to come up with five ideas is a form of individual brainstorming that happens when the group is together.

Silent brain writing needs no special materials other than some lined paper or paper divided into a number of equal sized boxes. Have everyone print the question or subject at the top. A question is always best because it opens one's mind to think about options and possibilities.

Encourage everyone to come up with a specific number of ideas related to the question or subject. Then pass the list in any direction that will keep the sheets moving around smoothly.

Each person then must read what is on the list they received and add five more, either by adding to one already there or coming up with something new. They can't repeat something on the list and can't repeat something they already wrote on another list. Pass the sheets again until they are full. You can decide if you want the participants to start a new sheet every time they receive a filled in one or once the sheets are filled to stop.

The best creative challenge is to require a larger number than you think is needed. If everyone can easily think of five then they must come up with 10. This is really important because the first few ideas thought of are always the same old ones that always come to mind. The Facilitator must challenge everyone to get those down on paper so they have to think differently, out-of-the-box, more creatively.

What to do after collecting all the filled in sheets

At this point divide into teams and start sorting the ideas into categories to discuss, mind map or brainstorm further as to how they could work.

Brainstorming with a Large Audience

Brainstorming with a large group requires some techniques to make everyone feel they are part of the process, to collect everyone's ideas, and to be able to share those ideas as quickly as possible with the whole group.

One method is to take turns having one person give an idea from their own list. Then challenge everyone in the audience to write down five ideas that that one idea brings to mind for them. Surprisingly there will be very few repeats. Multiply 5 by the number in your audience and you will have a large number of ideas added to the list.

Separating the Wheat from the Chaff: Some Ideas Keep Generating More Ideas

Once you have individual ideas, post five at a time in front of the group and ask members to expand on one or all of the ideas listed. Have someone other than the person who came up with idea do the expanding, even if they take it in a completely different direction than was meant by the person who wrote it down. This often leads to the expansion of ideas in new directions. You can still go back to explore the original directions as well. After 10 minutes, move on to the next five individually created ideas. This is piggybacking. Continue to sort through and expand on ideas. Those that are worthwhile will eventually stand out because they continue to reveal possibilities and greater applications.

 STORM SESSION 6

Julia Tesser stared intensely at the report that lay on her desk. Her gaze was so intense that she half expected the paper to burn.

The report detailed the corporate decision to begin expanding into rapidly developing countries: India and China to be first. In terms of telecommunication networks, it was complicated but doable. In her gut, however, Julia had a funny feeling about these plans.

She went over the report again. It said that a study of comparable American enterprises (e.g., McDonald's and KFC) had been conducted for three years and the findings substantiated a presence in these places.

Julia grabbed her pen and wrote on the back page, "I am concerned that such a quintessentially American brand cannot help become corrupted when owned and operated in an Oriental culture. I want to suggest that we either withdraw from the idea of such expansion, or draw up new guidelines that allow each franchise owner to contribute to décor, menu and location."

"What is my question?" she asked herself.

Grabbing her pen again she wrote, "My question is: how can I communicate my thoughts the most effectively to . . . (She looked at the report again and wrote down the author's name) Roberto Maxwell."

On another piece of paper Julia wrote:

"G.Q." She found that it was easier for her to imagine what G.Q. would say than it was to tell herself to think in a detailed fashion.

Half muttering to herself out loud, Julia wrote, "G.Q. would say, 'Send a persuasive and highly researched letter to Mr. Maxwell and include an offer to meet with him.

"Find demographic market research on the cultural and economic aspects of introducing alien culture products into an established and traditional society.

Discuss the risk factors vs. the success factors.

Working quickly, Julia wrote, "Miles" at the top of another page.

Here, she wrote: "The macro economies in developing countries are simply too weak to insure long-term success for franchises in these countries."

Julia then made a page for Anthony and wrote: "Go out and ask 100 India born residents living in a populated area if they would frequent an American coffee shop franchise. Do the same in China. I think you will find that the people of these countries hold tightly to the communal gathering places and to their particular ceremonies of drinking coffee together. Overlaying American style retail coffee shops could create hostility and consequently generate very little revenue."

Ahhh! She leaned back in her chair. Well, it was a start, a good start, and it only took her 20 minutes.

Julia looked out her window at the rain just starting to come down, and she felt an enormous release of tension. She speed-dialed her husband at his import office. "Hi Hon. Can we schedule some time tonight to go over an idea I want to present?"

Johnny, her husband, readily agreed and Julia placed the report in her briefcase and got back to the pile of papers on her desk. Later she would sit down with Miles, Anthony and G.Q. and get their input.

YOUR PERFECT STORM

Turn on your radio.

The question to find a variety of solutions is:

"What is the best, most effective way of thinking about doing business in developing countries if you are based in the United States of America?"

Wait for a song to begin and write down 30 possible answers during the song. When the song stops playing, stop writing.

Remember to step into the four different modes of thinking: Rational, Big Picture, Interpersonal and Organized.

"Business leaders know that heterogeneous workforces are rich seedbeds for ideas. Yet companies rarely tap employees for insights and experiences specific to their cultures."

~ Frans Johansson in Harvard Business Review article "Masters of the Multicultural" October 2005

Chapter 10

Go For Diversity!

"The problem is, innovation can't just be mandated from the top. Companies have the difficult task of forming internal cultures of innovations"

MARK VICKERS, HUMAN RESOURCE INSTITUTE

The Mediator
by Will Bullas, with permission of the artist. www.willbullas.com

So often when going into a new company as a computer salesperson, I was struck at how alike the individuals working there were. It is human nature to hire and select as team members people like us. Many studies have proven, however, that the more diverse a workforce or internal team is, the greater the success rate they have. In other words, companies make more money when they have a diverse group of people. Why? The reason is that tension between different perspectives leads to greater creativity in problem solving.

So, though we may feel more comfortable surrounded by individuals who look and think like us, the truth is that that comfort level comes at a price. Consider the alternative, creating affinity. Affinity is a feeling of belonging or of being alike. Creating affinity is the process of meeting someone, getting to know them a little bit and then finding something that you have in common with them and building on that to establish a relationship.

When we create affinity, we can experience not only financial benefits but also personal expansion as we grow in tolerance and understanding.

Below are basic tips to keep in mind as you are assembling or joining a brainstorming team:

- Accept ambiguity and diversion
- More diversity improves the results
- Vary your techniques to avoid boredom and mental blocking
- Note every idea including those that come up after the session is over
- Take breaks
- Mix up the teams
- Build quantity to achieve quality

If you are lucky you can choose the size and members of the team. Five to 12 is an ideal size. Go for diversity. By that, I mean diversity of thinking styles. Think about the people you know and how they view the world and make decisions. The more different they are, the better they are for your brainstorming project.

Go for diversity of knowledge about your project or question. If everyone has been working together on the same project it is unlikely that they will come up with ideas very different from each other. Consider perhaps a customer or two, perhaps someone from engineering, one from manufacturing and one from sales. How about someone from customer service who hears what customers complain about and ask for?

Go for diversity of age and number of years in your industry or company.

Go for other diversities if available and appropriate, such as different countries of origin, different first languages, and different ethnicity.

Balance

Balance for the purpose of achieving great ideas and profitable innovation requires as many of the following diversities on your team as possible:

Diversity in

1. Roles in the company (including a customer),
2. Number of years in the job
3. Age
4. Background, experiences
5. Skills
6. Education level and discipline, Subjects studied in school
7. Interests, hobbies
8. Books and movies preferred
9. Departments where they work
10. Outlook
11. Connections
12. Reasoning
13. Work methods
14. Decision processing preferences
15. Previous job
16. Language, and
17. Anything else you can think of whether or not it would seem to apply to the question at hand.
18. As well as the traditional definitions of diversity: race, gender, and country of origin.
19. And most of all, diversity of thinking styles[1].

Two people can observe the same event and describe it totally differently. We know this from many situations such as when police question witnesses or when a husband and wife discuss some previous event they both took part in, sometimes even their own wedding. So just the fact that you have multiple minds working on an issue, you will have some diversity. Upping the number of elements of diversity will escalate the viewpoints, ideas, and results.

STORM SESSION 7

"What are we doing?" G.Q. hunched down slightly in his seat on the van and let his cheek touch the cold glass. "I'm all for brainstorming and doing what it takes, but do we have to go on field trips in big vans just like tots?"

"It is rather . . . inconvenient," Julia sighed as she eased her large frame into the seat across from him. "At the same time, it's an adventure. Let's face it, I don't lead a very adventurous life, so this is interesting."

"My life is full of ceremonially attired soldiers and reenacted slaughter. I don't need adventure," G.Q. said refusing to budge from his position.

"Alright people!" Amy Ann turned to face everyone. "I hear rumblings and grumblings." She smiled enthusiastically. "This is what happens when people start to take you seriously. You have to travel, mix it up with other populations, inject diverse perspectives. Brainstorming at its best is all about mix and remix. You know that."

"Besides," she continued, this is going to be a lot of fun. I promise."

"Why do I feel like a cub scout?" G.Q asked.

Amy Ann paused, looking for the right retort but Miles came to her rescue, "Would it help if we were towing a cannon and going on horseback?"

Anthony raised his hand, "I didn't get all the details. Sorry. I just got back from vacation. I know we're going to the customer service call center and sales office, right?"

"Right," Amy Ann nodded. We have a room reserved next door, and we'll be meeting with four call agents, four franchise account managers and four outside sales agents. So, if you want to start individual brainstorming now on the way over, here are clipboards and paper for your personal use. The question is already written at the top of the page. It is:

"What feedback mechanisms can we put in place to capture customer experiences and lifestyle needs from customers and from point-of-sale employees?"

For the next 30 minutes, the group was quiet, writing in quick spurts and then pausing after a few minutes to look up at the roof of the van or out the window in deep introspection.

As the van pulled up to the hotel next door to the call center, they had to wait for another van in front of them to finish unloading a conga drum set and several guitar cases.

Trailing after their fearless Facilitator, Julia, Miles, G.Q. and Anthony rode the elevator up to the second floor and walked into an enormous ballroom.

Round tables with chairs and laptops were set up at one end of the room. A wide video screen had already been pulled down and a technician was completing a cable connection when they entered.

"Please pass me your ideas and then have a seat, one person at each table," Amy Ann handed the sheets to a young man who appeared at her elbow. Simon, please enter these. Simon walked to a laptop stage left and began typing. As he typed, the words appeared on the large screen.

"The Culture is Changing."

"Cool!" Miles was impressed. This was their first session together since Amy Ann had been promoted to full-time Facilitator and upper management had added brainstorming to the team's job descriptions. The new duties had come with the promise of sessions in exotic locales like Hawaii, Puerto Rico and even London. Miles had thought the inclusion of London rather odd until he recalled that the company had more stores in London than in any American city.

The doors to the ballroom opened and 12 individuals walked in rather sheepishly. Amy Ann met them and assigned one person from each job description to a table.

She then took the mike like a pro. "Thank you all for being here. As you know, we need to conform our business model more to the customer's lifestyle, the customer being two classes: 1) franchise owners and 2) the general public who purchase product.

Our concern is the high number of franchise defaults in the last two years. She pointed to the screen where the question stood out in three-foot letters.

I'm going to ask the people at each table to team up. I want you to give me a name for your team. You have two minutes to decide on a team name.

The team names, once chosen, appeared on the screen:

1. Rambo Players
2. The Knock Outs
3. The Beatles
4. Mind Masters

"OK. Ladies and Gentlemen. As you know, we don't have time for chit chat. In the next eight minutes, I want your team to generate 100, you heard me, 100 ways to capture customer experiences and lifestyle needs -- fifty for franchise owners and 50 for product buyers. Pass the pink paper to your right, write your idea on it or add to an idea already there, and keep going. When you're finished, type your answers into the laptop. On your mark, get set, go!"

Sudden silence descended upon the space. Except for paper sliding across tabletop and pens scratching, no sound could be heard.

"Stop!" Amy Ann held up her arm like a referee. "Please pass your sheets of paper to Simon who will collect them. Now, while we're waiting for Simon to cluster the results for us, Amy Ann pushed a button on a small device in her hand and the screen rose up to reveal a conga band. They began to play as Amy Ann called out, "Come on people, let's dance!"

Gradually, stiffly and with shyness the team members made their way out onto the dance floor. Amy Ann and a new, swarthy looking man with bulging biceps began leading a conga procession. The band picked up the pace and within a few minutes everyone was circling the room in time to the beat. The swarthy gentleman, who turned out to be a dance instructor, then led everyone in a quick samba lesson. Miles was not impressed and except for the conga line, refused to dance.

After half an hour, the group returned to their posts, flushed and energized.

On the screen, Simon had entered three main categories:

- One-on-one conversations
- Measurement of trials and tests
- Evaluation of service issues received via phone and Web

Four hundred ways to capture feedback plus the individual brainstorming responses from the van trip were all listed. Some of the one-on-one conversation ideas included:

- Asking customers why they came to the coffee shop, to work, to relax, to meet others.
- Asking customers what made them choose that coffee shop rather than another.
- Asking customers if they would still come to the coffee shop if it was operated by a different company • sold soup and sandwiches only • offered massages • shut down at five p.m. • played only country music • sold diabetic friendly products • had a singles night • let pets come in • had a play corner for children • had stars painted on the ceiling • had a guest appearance by Carly

Simon • had sheepskin rugs and pillows • had a storyteller for adults • had karaoke • flew the American flag out front • gave away a pair of sunglasses to the 100th customer • sold tattoo designs on the side • sold recording time in a studio on the side • sold life-size dolls of Alice in Wonderland and the Mad Hatter once a month before the Mad Hatter's tea • sold blackbird pies with plums in them • sold a chance to stand on a machine that gave you a full body reading: blood pressure, cholesterol, sugar, T-cell count, minerals etc. • sold palm readings • sold magic 8 balls • sold crystal balls • sold tap dance shoes and lessons • sold flowers • sold flower wreaths • crowns, chains • corsages • mums and bridal bouquets • sold flower car smell • sold lottery drawings for free cars • sold a new tire for $2 with 200 cups of coffee • sold a ride on a sleeper train • sold airline tickets for one-tenth the regular price but sealed in envelopes and you had to take what you got • sold Victoria's Secret items inside of sealed coffee cups • sold espresso machines and trips to Italy • sold fine wine • coffee • cheese and bread in pretty picnic baskets • sold coffee in little carts on the street • in trucks in neighborhoods • in beauty salons • in car repair places • in hospital parking lots • at school dances • at craft shows • at horse shows • at beauty contests • at shoe stores • at Home Depots • at drug stores like old fashioned drug store lunch counters.

The trials were extensive, and then the complaint measurement was less extensive.

In one hour, the group had sifted through the ideas with Amy Ann to three more categories just for one-on-one conversations with product buying customers. These were:

- Convenience– in a place where you have to wait or go for errands
- Enjoyment – providing a service or product you like a lot
- Financial – Giving you an opportunity to save money on a large ticket item

As you can see, the group gradually began to nail down real possibilities that conformed to customer lifestyles and went above and beyond just the products currently offered in the setting of a coffee shop.

The inclusion of customer service people, sales agents and franchise account managers gave the brainstorming session an injection of diverse perspectives. As they rode back to the office on the van, Julia, Miles, G.Q. and Anthony were all mulling over their expanded understandings of the business.

"I'm so glad we did this," Anthony said to Amy Ann.

"Yes," G.Q. agreed. I learned a lot from the sales agents especially. I didn't know that the training process was so extensive and time-consuming."

"And I didn't know," said Miles, "that the average customer spends less than 15 minutes, and $5.00 or less, in the store. I had a picture of people hanging out, which is only true of two percent."

"I really enjoyed the dance lesson myself," Amy Ann's cheeks were tanned and glowing.

She cleared her throat and regained a professional poise." We're gradually refining new approaches. I'm realizing that a consistent practice of brainstorming across the organization is a huge task. Already, though, I think management is seeing that its people can generate more profits through their imaginations than they ever....imagined." She giggled.

Miles settled into his seat with resignation. He knew what it meant when a young woman giggled soon after dancing with someone. He sighed. Amy Ann was too elusive, too caught up in brainstorming and samba-ing with beefy guys. She was just out-of-reach. She was just out of his reach. He looked out the window and began to count bumper stickers on passing cars.

YOUR PERFECT STORM

Gather four people together as your brainstorming team. Write down the following information about each person:

1. Job
2. Primary interests and hobbies
3. First language
4. Thinking style
5. Place of birth
6. Age

Now, think of four more people that you could ask to join the group who do not share any of the qualities of the first four, as far as you know. You may have to scan employee rosters, or look online for names of people in different positions in your company. The important thing is to seek out difference, identify it and learn to accept and attract diversity into your sphere of activity.

1.

2.

3.

4.

Name two friends that you have who do not share at least three of the following with you:

- Education level
- Race
- Age
- Hobbies or interests
- Marital status

Name two people at your workplace whom you don't know well, who are different from you in three or more ways (from the list above), and with whom you will try to create an affinity in the next week.

1.

2.

Chapter 11

When Minds Click: Collaborative Brainstorming Power

"Competence is the enemy of change."

SETH GODIN, AUTHOR, FORMER FAST COMPANY COLUMNIST, FROM HIS ARTICLE "CHANGE AGENT"

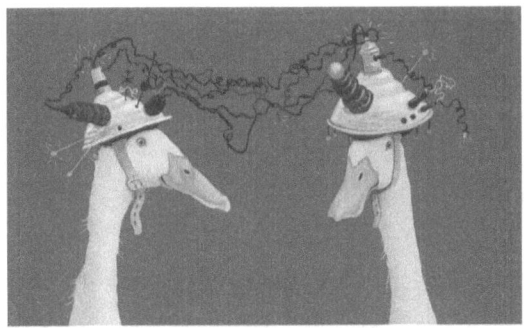

A Meeting of the Minds
by Will Bullas, with permission of the artist. www.willbullas.com

What you can accomplish brainstorming on your own increases exponentially when you are able to bring a strong, diverse team together to spend time brainstorming and build on each other's ideas. So far, we have talked about thinking styles such as Big Picture or Organized, but I want to point out that thinking styles are different from intelligences. Intelligence is an innate ability, while thinking style is the way you organize ideas. A person with a high interpersonal intelligence may have a Big Picture thinking style or he or she may have an Organized thinking style. (Find more information on multiple intelligences in the last chapter.)

When putting together a diverse brainstorming group, you want to find people who figuratively live in parallel universes from each other. I'm talking about individuals with such widely varied backgrounds and experience with life and with the topic at hand that they astound one another just by speaking or being the same room.

Keep certain pointers in mind when assembling your group. Most people tend to have friends very much like themselves. They tend to dress alike, eat alike and think alike, so right there you know that if you have two potential participants from the same group who are good friends that one of them is probably a good enough representative.

Work especially hard to bring in racial and socio-economic variety to your group.

When bringing different types of thinkers together, you want to find people who are diverse in terms of:

1. Experience with the topic: The closer someone is to the topic, the harder it will be to see it from totally different perspectives. But you also need some representation from those most knowledgeable, asking them to be careful not to dominate the session, just making notes in the beginning. Also find somebody who has little or no preconceived knowledge of the topic so they are forced to ask a lot of naïve questions.

2. Types of intelligence: Howard Gardner's multiple intelligences theory advises attracting people whose intelligences stand out in different categories. According to Gardner, the seven intelligences are Linguistic, Logical-Mathematical, Musical, Bodily-Kinesthetic, Spatial, Interpersonal, and Intrapersonal. Normally they don't operate independently. Instead they work together and complement each other. However, you probably know people who display preponderance in one or another of

the seven intelligences. When you can add this diversity it will enrich the whole brainstorming experience and result.

In school we all took intelligence tests that labeled us based on an IQ measurement. In life and in business in general, many intelligences other than math and science are much more helpful in the business world. For example, being able to read other people's feelings is an important intelligence to have, but it is neither measured nor taught. Other intelligences include being able to see and reflect beauty, perhaps realized in creating surroundings that help people work better. When we start to recognize that in life there are a number of different ways that a person can be intelligent, then we have a more holistic way of doing business.

In an ideal world we would try to hire a good mix of thinking styles and intelligences to create wonderful diversity on our team. In reality we can't always test people beforehand. What I suggest is that you bring out abilities and differences in the group that you have.

Perhaps you don't have the luxury of a large pool of people from which to choose. In that case, use specific processes in the meeting that can bring out the different ways of seeing the world.

For instance, you might ask, "How can we work with this product in a way to attract people who care about their relationships with other people? How would someone who is deeply attracted to beauty respond to this? What kind of product or service would light up the sky for someone who relates at a kinesthetic energy level?"

You can ask questions that attract different intelligences, or you can invite people with specific types of intelligence. Obviously, inviting people who work in diverse areas increases the likelihood that they have different types of intelligence. A welder, an arborist and a newborn infant caregiver would likely bring multiple and differing intelligences to the brainstorming session. Most people choose a profession that fits their interests and natural skills and intelligence, if they can.

Oftentimes you will find that individuals have tried to bring out different parts of themselves but didn't feel that they were valued by other people when they did. For example, an engineer with a high spatial intelligence may have taken several drawing classes or studied sculpture but found that his other logical-mathematical intelligence friends didn't "get it." During a brainstorming session, people with a real variety of intelligences may keep their ideas to themselves. Some people are more willing to share and express their ideas than others if they're in a culture that encourages that, they do. If the person has a thinking style that acquiesces to others you must ask yourself the question, "How do I bring out all of the different intelligences in these people?" We want to recognize different intelligences, even if they are latent, and help people bring them out.

Set up in advance 20 questions with multiple-choice answers and pass them out on a piece of paper so no one feels intimidated. One question might be: Angel came home from school and one of his socks was bright red. The other one was white. His mother said, "What happened to your sock?" Have the participants answer the question as if they were the little boy. The different types of intelligence are: Linguistic, Logical-Mathematical, Musical, Bodily-kinesthetic, Spatial, Interpersonal, and Intrapersonal.

Here are some examples of answers from different intelligence types. Angel said:

A. All the kids wore two different colored socks today for the big game. (Logical-Mathematical Intelligence)
B. Jeremy's sock got dog 'poop' on it. The teacher only had one spare and it was red. Jeremy didn't want to wear two different colors. It seemed like fun so I did it for him. (Intrapersonal Intelligence.)
C. I wore one red sock because the last two times I did it Daddy talked to me a lot after he got home from work. Is he home yet? (Interpersonal Intelligence)

I teach a course called "Critical Thinking" at the American Management Association. I often refer to it as "Creativity and Critical Thinking" but I always need to explain the word *creative*. Many business people think they are not creative and often think it is not necessary. The truth is that if we don't have our creative side operating, we cannot be good critical thinkers. This is one of the values of brainstorming and the rationale for having people in your group who are strongly creative on different planes of intelligence.

 STORM SESSION 8

Anthony caught sight of Amy Ann sitting at the desk in the main lobby. He sidled up behind her and whispered, "What are you doing? I thought you were a brainstorming Facilitator now."

Amy Ann started and let out a little scream. "Anthony! You scared me!"

"So sorry." Anthony grinned to show that he had rather enjoyed scaring her.

I just want to meet a few people from different backgrounds to invite to be on the team."

"What's the next session going to be about?"

"That's for me to know and you to find out," Amy batted her eyelashes at Anthony. "Now, go away!"

"Humph. You're no fun." Anthony walked away laughing.

Just then a thin Asian woman with long parted hair twisted up in a bun entered the giant glass doors. Her print dress was a beautiful design of interwoven orchids. Amy Ann stepped up to her.

"Excuse me." She stuck out her hand. "My name is Amy Ann Wainthrop, and I'm the new Brainstorming Facilitator. We're looking for new people to bring fresh perspectives to the group. May I ask you a few questions?"

The woman nodded, "Of course."

"Well, first of all, what is your name?"

"Daisy Ticoshi."

"Your title?"

"Artist designer. I design the light fixtures, tables, chairs, buildings sometimes, cups… you name it."

"Where are you from Daisy?"

"Japan. I studied art and architecture in Paris and have lived in the United States for five years."

Amy Ann put her clipboard down. "Would you be interested in joining our group next Thursday?" She handed Daisy her card. If you would email me, I'll send you a meeting invitation."

Daisy looked intrigued. "So you want my ideas?"

"Yes, that's it."

Daisy looked at Amy Ann's card curiously. "What is the subject??

"I'll let you know either a few hours beforehand or at the meeting."

Daisy shrugged. "OK. It might be fun."

"Brainstorming sessions are a lot of fun!" Amy Ann enthused, "But they're work too. No worries. You'll love it." She shook Daisy's small, delicate hand and watched her go through the main doors and into the maze of offices.

Within minutes, a tall auburn-haired woman passed thought the lobby. She stood around six feet tall and wore a demure navy silk blazer with a long matching skirt. Amy Ann approached the woman with a big smile. Immediately the woman's face lit up with a grin outlined in orange lipstick.

Amy Ann explained her mission, and the woman, Georgia, seemed almost grateful at the prospect of contributing to a brainstorming session. She said, "I was just telling myself on the way in today that I really needed to add some creativity to my life."

"What sort of work do you do?" Amy Ann Asked, clipboard ready.

"I'm what you call a business analyst. Mostly I just fix broken code." She smiled again. "I was one of the first female programmers on the block."

"Excellent!" Amy Ann made a notation. "Would you be interested in participating in a brainstorming session?"

"Honey, you tell me the time and place, and I'll be there!" Georgia scooped Amy Ann's hands into her wide ones for a few seconds and then glided through the large double doors. "I'm the only Georgia in the directory!" she called out. "You can't miss me!"

Congratulating herself on two successful encounters in a short period of time, Amy Ann was ready to call it a day. She walked out of the main building and along the south side towards her office door. Almost hidden in the shadow of an old sycamore, she saw a man sitting at a picnic table in the grassy courtyard. He was wearing a tan shirt, the type that machine operators and park employees sometimes wear. In the late morning light, Amy Ann saw that he had rather longish swept back blond hair, and a handsome face. He was reading a thick book and eating tacos.

Pulling out her pen and paper again, Amy Ann approached the man. He looked up at her with calm blue eyes. "I'm sorry to disturb you," she began. Would you mind if I asked you a few questions for a survey I'm doing?"

He smiled shyly. "Sure."

"Well, my name is Amy Ann Wainthrop, and I'm trying to find different types of people who work for this company. I'm planning brainstorming meetings, and one of the things we need are different perspectives."

"OK." He was not a big talker.

"What's your name?"

"My name is John Smith. Most of my friends call me Smitty."

"Smitty. Hmm, that's an interesting nickname."

Smitty nodded, "It's in reference to my trade…my former trade. I used to be a farrier, a person who puts shoes on horses. We have to pound out the metal sometimes, and that's where the "Smitty" reference comes from."

"Horses? You're a long way from a horse now," Amy Ann noted wryly.

"Yep." He motioned towards the parking lot. "The riding stables all around my area laid off and closed up. Sold the horses off to people in Florida and California mostly. My sister, Agnes, gave me her car to stay in and drive around until I find work. I've been here now about a week."

"You live in your car?"

"Yep. For the time being. It's a big ol' Caddy. Plenty of room for me. I'm used to just a bunk in the tack room."

"What sort of work are you doing here?"

"Maintenance. I can fix anything but I'm not a certified electrician…yet." He grinned and looked down at the book.

"Thank you so much Smitty," Amy Ann smiled and shook his hand. "I may be calling on you."

YOUR PERFECT STORM

Make a list of all the people on your team. Next to their name, write down their thinking style and types of intelligence. Also include their age and something about their background.

What can you surmise from looking at this information? What types of people are missing from your team? Make a list showing what sort of individuals you need.

Consider whom you know who works at your company. Do any of these people fit into the list you've made? If so, approach them and invite them to join the group.

Realize that you don't have to like the person; you just have to identify them and invite them to come to the next brainstorming session. Keep inviting people until you have at least three confirmations.

Chapter 12

Planning for a Brainstorming Session

*"Failure to plan is a plan for failure" (unknown)
. . . Easy for some to say, not so easy for others.*

© Alexey Shestakov - Fotolia.com

If people are not comfortable with this at first, they will need something to trigger the movement toward sharing lots of ideas. If you're in charge you need to have some things to get things rolling, such as card decks made for this purpose and brain writing materials. Plan to have supplies available and never do more than two tools in a meeting. If one is working don't stop to pull another one out.

If everyone is calling out ideas, how will you save all those ideas?

Focus on writing down every keyword, not every word. This is the best way to take notes. A keyword will later trigger the rest of the thought. That is why it is called a key-word. Mind mapping is an organized way to get all the keywords down and use connecting lines to pull the thoughts together.

As with most things in the business world, failing to plan is a plan for failure. Even though there are times that a situation comes up spontaneously and you need to brainstorm, when possible, plan based on the who?, what?, when?, where?, why?, and how? questions. These questions are your base or foundation.

Planning for a Brainstorming Meeting

When your brainstorming meetings can be planned ahead, you can prepare materials and expectations. You can also ask everyone to come ready with some ideas based on a question you pose.

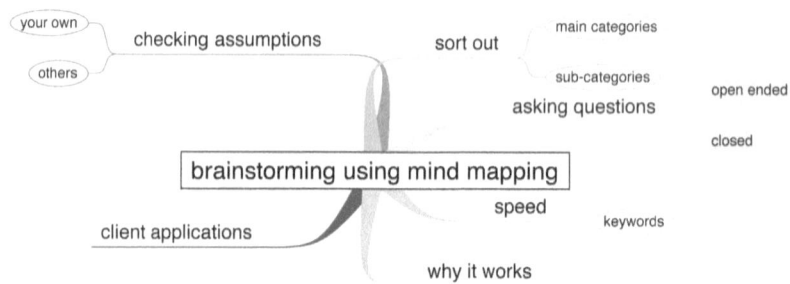

1. Let the team know what the topic or question is going to be.
2. Assign everyone the task to bring at least three (or a number that you pick) ideas to get things started.
3. Everyone writes the ideas on separate sticky notes, 3x5 cards, or the first lines of a brain-writing sheet.

4. Develop a mind map, or divide the group and give each team one cluster of ideas to expand.
5. Develop a list of options; spend time expanding the option list.
6. Do a draft prioritization of the options.
7. Take the first three or four on the list and do a pro and con list for each of them.
8. Decide whether to implement one or more.
9. Put a basic implementation plan in place in which everyone has a piece and there is a leader.
10. Go for it!

Spontaneous Brainstorming in a Meeting

> "We can't solve problems by using the same kind of thinking we used when we created them."
> ~ Albert Einstein[1]

Often a subject, question, or problem is discussed in a meeting and someone says, "Let's brainstorm it!" Then the meeting turns into a brainstorming meeting, and you did not have time to prepare. Having some brainstorming tools and processes that you can access quickly can make the session successful.

What usually follows is that a person goes to a board or flip chart and asks for ideas. A list is developed and a discussion follows. Unfortunately, always doing brainstorming the same way gets the same results, and people get bored. They look around for someone else to suggest something. Here are some solutions to these typical problems:

1. Start by being sure the subject or problem is understood and everyone agrees. Then write it down as an open-ended question.
2. Next, use one of the individual methods to have everyone write as many ideas as they can come up with. (See individual methods for a number of ideas how to do this.) Encourage everyone to write down everything that comes to mind even if they think it sounds silly, or that it wouldn't work. Great ideas often come from expanding on an idea that might have been previously discarded. No negativity and no value judgments, even positive ones, at this point. Brain-writing or chal-

lenging everyone to come up with five ideas can get things started. The best creative challenge is to require a larger number than you think is needed. If everyone can easily think of five then challenge them to come up with 10. This is really important because the first few ideas thought of are always the same old ones that always come to mind. You must challenge everyone to get those down on paper, so they have to move on to think different, out of the box, more creatively.

Tools with questions posed such as the KnowBrainer® Whackpack®, and Thinkpak® can be used though often they aren't needed until the next step.

3. Gather all the ideas, clustering them by topic. Use mind mapping, sticky-note clusters, affinity diagram (silent organizing of topics by a group), or dividing up teams to work further on each cluster. Expand the lists of ideas and don't allow value judgments. I am repeating this because it is so important and is so often ignored:

Value judgments stop the contribution of ideas even if they are positive ones.

We know that negative value judgments will stop people from continuing to contribute ideas, but so will positive remarks. A positive remark may make it seem like the group has an answer or solution, and they can all stop. Even when someone has some more ideas to contribute when comments make it sound like you are done they hold back.

4. Use the ideas and clusters to come up with more ideas, ideas that piggyback on ones already written, and combinations. Ask an open-ended question about each idea and see where that leads.

This is a great time to bring out one of the tools to trigger more questions.

"Never stop questioning."

1. If you must come up with a decision in this meeting, then start organizing the clusters of ideas into options without narrowing down to one answer. Prioritize the options. Look at the pros and cons of each of the options. Ask more open-ended questions about the options you are considering. Ask "What if?" questions. Ask "Why not?" questions.

Don't jump to a conclusion too quickly, or you may choose one that is not as good as another on the list.

2. If you can take some more time, give everyone a small pad of paper that they must keep with them at all times until your follow-up meeting, even if the meeting is later the same day or the next morning. On that pad they should keep writing more ideas and thoughts about the subject. The pad of paper and a flashlight should be put on the bed stand at night since often we come up with our best ideas while dreaming, and they must be written down immediately. We always think we will remember in the morning but seldom are able to. Just write it down!

3. Choose or decide on one or more of the options to implement. Save the notes since the other options may be of value in the future.

Always:

Have fun

Understand what you are trying to accomplish

Accept ambiguity and diversion

More diversity improves the results

Vary your techniques to avoid boredom and mental blocking

Note every idea including those that come up after the session is over

Take breaks

Mix up the teams

Looking for both quantity and quality

What

Determine what will be the subject or question. Keep returning to it if the conversation or ideas seem to be diverging. Make sure that you make a note of the divergent ideas, even if they seem unconnected to the question. You may discover later that they popped up for a reason. Also it shows respect to the contributor and allows you to quickly get the session refocused.

When

Plan the session when everyone invited can set aside the time and feel relaxed about working on the issue. Though playfulness and lightheartedness helps ideas flow more smoothly, this is a serious business question you are addressing, and everyone must know that the results will be used to make business decisions and measured by ROI (both Return on Ideas and Return on Investment).

Why

Be clear about why you need the subject explored in new ways. Some subjects may be obvious, such as a problem that has not been solved using your usual methods, and now it needs innovative solutions.

Also be clear that the goal is to have as many ideas as possible, not just a list of obvious ones. So the purpose at first is quantity, not quality. Quality happens because the process of sifting and combining, when you have a large quantity of ideas, allows the group to improve the results.

Where

Find a place that doesn't feel like your usual office or conference room. Some companies have created rooms with couches or colorful tables. Solution People[1] makes everyone take off their shoes and put on socks that they provide. Most places include toys or interesting pictures or objects around the room.

You need a place free of outside interference or noise so that everyone can concentrate on the subject at hand.

How

Here are two important starting steps:

1. Understand the subject or question. Discuss why you are working on new and different ways of looking at the subject. Talk about what will likely be done with the results.
2. Give everyone, (or if it just you) plenty of blank paper. Write the question or topic at the top. Start writing as many ideas as fast as possible without discussing them. There are some specific alternate ways to do this step listed in a later chapter, but for now just understand the concept. You want everyone to write down as many things as they can think of before anyone else can censor with a look or comment. You

do it fast so your own brain can't censor. And you challenge them with a big number so that it forces everyone to work fast.

What to do when you feel burned out and out of ideas?

Take a break. It could be a physical break -- go for a walk, get a drink of water, go home and sleep on it.

It could be a different approach. Use a different brainstorming method. Go from team brainstorming to working individually, or from working individually to finding a few others with whom to work.

If you have many interesting objects around the room, pick one up at random and ask how does this relate? What analogy could we make between our product, approach, or problem?

Or it could be a mental break. Change the subject. Work on something else for a while. Get something else done and come back to this subject in 45 minutes or the next morning. Always keep a small pad of paper and pen with you. When you start thinking about something else, ideas will come popping into your head about the subject where you were stymied. Write them down immediately. No matter how sure you are that you will remember this great idea later, you won't. Something will take your thoughts in a different direction, and all you will remember is that you had a great idea. So be prepared and write it down right away.

Find a new viewpoint or perspective

Ask how your mother or father would view the issue. What would they ask?

How would a child think about it? Someone who didn't speak your language? Your competitor? A customer? Someone who knows nothing about your company? Someone with only a sixth grade education? What do you think people will say 20 years from now looking back? How would your ancestors have solved the problem?

What assumptions have you made?

Which assumptions may not be true? Which assumptions have you made that others may not have made? What if the opposite were true? What if you couldn't make that assumption?

When you brainstorm in a group, it tends to feel like a joint decision.

 STORM SESSION 9

Executive Understanding of Brainstorming Planning

The Outlook software program on her desktop made a beeping sound. Amy Ann didn't need to look at the appointment to know that it was: a meeting with Theo, Arjun and Madeline.

They wanted to have a meeting with her about the brainstorming sessions.

Amy Ann walked down the hallway to the Pound Cake room.

"So what if they're big shots," she told herself. "They're just people. Now is not the time to be caught up in politics." As she opened the door, she cleared her throat self-consciously.

"Here she is!" Arjun stood up and motioned to her to have a seat at the round table.

Theo and Madeline nodded and said hello to her.

"Amy Ann, the reason we wanted to meet with you is to gather information from you about the basic process of creating a brainstorming session. We're interested in continuing these and possibly replicating them at our overseas offices. So, what we want to do is ask you to walk us through the steps you take, and then we'll ask a few questions. So, what do you do first?"

Amy Ann nodded and finished sorting through her papers. She had come prepared with various lists.

"First of all, I get a question or a set of questions, as you know because you've been sending them to me.

"Now, depending on the question, I figure out where and how to conduct the session. For instance, if the question is taking a previous question to a deeper level, then I might want to use visual aides like playing cards or photos or even slides to stimulate even deeper associations. If it's a new question or a short question, I might just rely on a round robin or timed writing exercise."

"This is interesting," Arjun noted. "What sort of equipment and supplies do you normally have on hand?"

"I always have something to record the responses. It may be a big white board, a large tablet or a black board. If we don't have those things, perhaps notebook computers, a tablet or a digital recorder.

"The second thing I like to generally have at a session is food. It's not necessary, but I've noticed that it seems to loosen people up when they eat together. It depends. Sometimes, I create a tense, time-sensitive atmosphere with low lighting and rhythmic music. In this way, I don't want the group to be loose, but to be very focused and a bit on edge. It depends again on the question, how many people are in the group, and if the question is a "drill-down" from an earlier question or a new one."

"You mentioned music?" Theo prodded.

"Sure, both music and movement can be vital in keeping bodies awake and enthusiastic."

"Well, that's what I was wondering," Theo interjected. "I mean, don't people get tired of it all and burned out?"

Amy Ann smiled. "You know, they do, but at the same time, it's so invigorating to have the management in your company solicit your input. You can imagine how fulfilling it is for an employee to feel as if their ideas are valued – even the slightly weird and crazy ones."

"Overall," she continued, " I would say that the most important aspect of a brainstorming session is making sure that people move quickly, because this way they push their brains to come up with new ideas.

"Also, that there is no commenting either positively or negatively regarding the ideas that are contributed."

"What do you mean?" Arjun asked.

"I mean that any judgment whatsoever that is expressed about an idea puts a damper on all of the other ideas. If you hear anything that makes you want to comment, just refrain from showing any reaction. That's the rule."

"What else?' Arjun asked.

"I think you have to really analyze the answers in different ways. I mean, think about each answer that you like from the perspective of a rational mind, a broad picture mind etc. I've made a list of thinking styles as well as a list of different types of intelligences. They're not the same thing exactly.[2] Employ as many perspectives as possible and ask as many who, what, why, when, and how questions that you can think of. I made a list of the questions for you."

Amy Ann handed out her packet of information.

"Finally, depending on the subject and the amount of time we have, we work as a team to first cluster the ideas into their natural groupings and then build a mind map or other written method so we can keep adding, following links that seem most fruitful, and then use the diagram to share and explain the results."

Madeline leaned back in her chair and smiled. "You know what I like about this brainstorming? It's not set in stone. I mean, it's not a strictly defined business process at this time. We can play with the practice. We can use it in small groups, large groups or as individuals. We can make it a company-wide experience or keep it contained in a specialized area. Brainstorming itself is flexible thinking inside of a guided, structured timeframe. It's really a very exciting, useful way to discover new ideas, create greater profits, but also to really…I don't know…tap into the resources of employees. As a CFO, I can sense that we've uncovered a gold mine."

"A gold mine?" Arjun looked puzzled.

"Do you mean the people are a gold mine…a greater resource than before brainstorming?" Theo helpfully suggested.

"Yes, that's what I mean. I mean that beyond specific skill sets, the people are contributing value to the company through these sessions."

"Ah. Yes. I do see what you're saying." Arjun laughed. "Of course you are seeing brainstorming from a spreadsheet point-of-view! You know," he shifted his attention to Amy Ann, "this didn't take as long as I thought. I think we already knew most of this from sitting in on sessions earlier, but we wanted to just check with you to be sure." He put his hand out to Amy Ann. "I thank you for your time, Amy Ann. I believe we've gotten a good picture of how the process works. Thank you especially for the printed materials."

"Oh, you're welcome," Amy Ann rose to her feet. "By the way, there's a great book on the subject of brainstorming. The title is something like *Power Brainstorming: Great Ideas at Lightning Speed*. I'll email you the exact reference if you'd like."

"Yes, please do."

Amy Ann shook hands with Theo, Arjun and Madeline and made her exit. Then, she remembered something and returned immediately to the meeting room.

"I'm sorry, I forgot to mention to you that changing environments, you know, can be very important if you're using the same group over a long period of time. Anyway, next week I had planned to take the core group to the park and do some rollerblading; maybe have a little picnic during our session. I don't have the full question yet, but I know it's a drill-down from previous ideas they generated. You're all invited."

The three executives looked both curious and cautious. Theo smiled. "I like that!

I'll be there."

"Great." Amy Ann nodded goodbye again and left the room.

YOUR PERFECT STORM

You are the superintendent of schools for a 3A school district. In the last six months, you've seen a dramatic climb in dropout rates among Spanish speaking students. You've consulted with the experts, talked to counselors and even gone to visit other school districts. Now, you want to see if the school employees: teachers, secretaries, janitors– everyone can contribute ideas to increase retention of this population.

Step 1.

Brainstorm in a fairly structured way what questions need to be answered about how to conduct the first session. If you don't use any structure, you may just list the questions, then it might look like this:

Write about the brainstorming sessions that you are going to schedule.

1. Where will they be held?
2. Who will attend?
3. How many people will be in each session?
4. When will they be held?
5. Who will facilitate?
6. What sort of tools will you use?
    Music _____
    Pictures_____
    Color _____
    Timed round robins _____
    Exercises_____
    Audio/video _____
    Software programs _____
7. What questions will you ask?
8. How many sessions will you schedule?
9. Would you ever include students? If so, how many and under what circumstances? _____
10. What about parents?_____
11. How far in advance will you schedule the meetings?

Step 2: How will you know when you have all the questions written down? If you give this brainstorming session some structure, such as the following, you are more likely to come up with all or most of the questions you need answered.

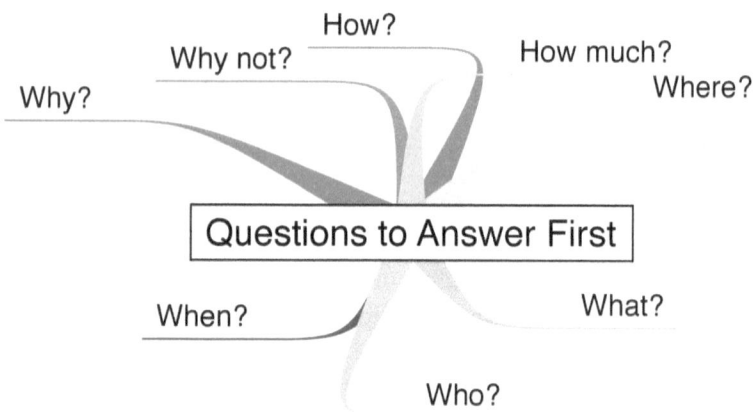

Fill in what else you would need to question before going on to step 2.

Step 2.

Divide the questions by labeling them into A, B, and C as described below:

  A. Facts you can find out
  B. Opinions and whose opinion will decide
  C. More complex questions that need some work to answer

Then you can go get the answers.

Now use the same technique for a meeting you are going to plan or could hypothetically plan for your business.

Chapter 13

Using Tools to Help Trigger Brainstorming Visual Thinking

ROI = Return on Ideas

Cats and Dogma
by Will Bullas, with permission of the artist. www.willbullas.com

Boost participation and idea-generation by using visual methods to enhance the brainstorming process.

Visual Thinking refers to any technique that allows you or your team to build on a visual concept of the ideas being generated and discussed.

How to Think Visually

1. Use the analogy of associations and connections between ideas. This is how your brain learns something new, stores it and retrieves it later. It has to have a connection to something else you know.
2. Visual thinking example: A mind map is a great way to connect ideas on paper, board, or screen so you can see the ideas *and* the connections.
3. Use color. Using multiple colors for your drawing invigorates your thought processes and attention. And I use the word drawing in a very loose way. Keywords and rough sketches, including stick figures are just fine. Thinking on paper or a board should be free and easy. There are books about how to draw simple symbols such as:
   - Visual Thinking: Tools for Mapping Your Ideas by Margulies and Valenza or
   - Beyond Words by Milly Sonneman: Learning and Teaching Visual Mapping

Whenever possible start any brainstorming mind maps by hand drawing. When you use markers and write fast and large on paper or a board, just letting it flow, ignoring any grammar or spelling interruptions, the ideas will flow out more easily. It helps in developing the big picture of the ideas and thoughts. The online programs are fantastic for sharing mind maps and other visual methods, but they can be restricting during the free flow stage because you have to deal with the technology and where to put items and notes.

Edward deBono uses color to represent different positions during a discussion in his book called *6 Hats and Other Brainstorming Methods*. He recommends that you stick to one position at a time in order to bring each one out as fully as possible.

- Organization and control
- Creativity and new ideas

- Positive thinking
- Objectivity or neutral position
- Feelings and emotions
- Caution, negatives.

Refer to any of his excellent books for more details (listed in the resource section) on how to use his methods in the brainstorming process.

4. The larger the space (paper or board) the more free you will feel vs. the size of a computer screen.
5. Then, during the review and organize stage, it is often helpful to put your results into a computer application program[1] designed to help you visualize. For some, it is helpful to work on a computer right from the start, especially if you can project what you are doing on a screen large enough for everyone to see.
6. Use pictures, drawings, shapes, clip art, historic photos, pictures of famous people -- all the images that you can think of that can stimulate thinking about your brainstorming subject. The pictures don't have to have anything to do with the subject. They just have to evoke other images and ideas to keep the brainstorming going.
7. Some of the brainstorming tools use pictures for this purpose. In all cases you ask the questions: What does this picture bring to mind? What does it have to do with our subject? If you knew there was a connection what could it be? Take two different pictures; explore how they could be connected and what that could mean for your brainstorming subject?
8. Word pictures: Take the words that are part of your brainstorming subject and use http://www.visualthesaurus.com to look at the words that come up. Click on one of the words and make it the center of a new search. Look at the big picture developing of the words that are connected. Click on the opposite word and explore it, too.

 STORM SESSION 10

Amy Ann looked at her brainstorming-planning checklist. She smiled, imagining how the group would like the park environment and the rollerblades they would need to get them to the right spot. Anticipating Julia's reluctance to rollerblade, she also had a back-up golf cart ready.

The cool breezes of spring, the flowers and butterflies would all serve as visual stimulants. In addition, Amy Ann had several sets of photographs and a deck of brainstorming visualization cards. (Several brands are listed in the Resource section at the end of the book). The session was scheduled to be two hours long, with 30 minutes for a recreational break. Miles was bringing a portable CD player, and Anthony was bringing a pan of his special tomato pies to welcome the new people. Amy Ann was glad to have regular brainstorming members pitching in with a sense of unity and ownership.

The question this time was one that would require all of their brains to be sharp, relaxed and flexible.

Thursday came, and all of the colorfully laced rollerblades arrived in everyone's size. The journey to the picnic tables went off without a hitch. Even G.Q. seemed to be enjoying himself.

Theo Wilson was part of the party again. Smitty was clearly thrilled to be there and had taken to sharing his bunkhouse jokes with Theo. Amy Ann considered if she should tell Smitty that Theo was a top-level executive. She decided to leave the facts to reveal themselves when the time was right.

Smitty stood still on a clump of buffalo grass and inhaled deeply. "A mare and a pony came through here early in the morning." His eyes scanned the ground in all directions for several minutes. "Yep. See here? Here are the hoof prints. Looks like the pony's in good shape but the mare's a little loose in the shoe." Amy Ann laughed good-humouredly.

"I guess you'll be applying your observation skills to wires and circuits pretty soon."

"Yes," he nodded his head slowly, while his eyes belied and infinitely faster process going on behind them. "Yes, as a matter-of-fact, I've got a little system worked out. It's complicated, but let's just say that when I see a rounded circuit with a wiring harness, I think of four Tennessee Walkers in bridle bits."

"That's great, Smitty! Actually, we'll be doing similar visual exercises today, so you should feel right at home."

"That so?" Smitty looked relieved. "That so?"

Fifteen minutes later, in front of the group. Amy Ann asked the question, "If our customers stopped coming to our stores because of gas, energy and other costs, what would we do? Would we keep selling our products? If so, how? If not, what new products or services would we sell? It could be anything.

After we come up with these answers, we'll go back and see if the new ideas have something fresh to offer our business now."

"Remember," Amy Ann gently prodded them, "This question comes in two parts: number one, how would we get product to customers if they didn't come into the shops? Today I'm going to show you a series of pictures, and you shout out at your turn any idea that you have."

She set the first picture of a window washer suspended over New York City, eating a bagel and drinking a cup of coffee. "We'll go around counter-clockwise and start with you, Daisy."

G.Q. spoke up, "For the record, I think this is a waste of time – this question. If they won't walk in, they're not going to shell out dough somewhere else."

"How can you be so sure?" Miles asked him. "It's worth a try."

G.Q. shrugged. "Whatever."

"OOOKaaay…" Amy Ann cleared her throat. "Once more from the top. I've gone over the guidelines. You now have seven to 10 seconds to shout out your answer. She pointed to Daisy who had been sitting quietly on her right.

Daisy blinked rapidly and whispered, "Delivery?"

Miles was next, "Coffee/bread trucks like ice cream trucks."

Smitty – "A service at every office, like bottled water."

Georgia – "A push cart on the corner, like they sell hot dogs."

G.Q. (yawning) – Brand in the grocery store.

Anthony – Sell at alternative fuel stations, like bio-diesel.

Theo – Deliver on trays to offices, like they do in Buenos Aires.

Julia – Automatic delivery every morning, like the milkman.

Daisy – Push a code into your cell phone and a courier finds you with coffee, etc.

Miles – Systematic delivery to every office and neighborhood without prior orders, just deliver and expect that they'll pay.

Smitty – Horse and carriage.

Georgia – Trained dogs with saddle pouches.

G.Q. – Elevators that have coffee bars inside of them.

Anthony – Call the stores "No Gyms" and also sell hot wings, queso[2] and beer.

Amy Ann called out, "Stop! OK we're getting into the second part of the question."

She put up a second picture of two black bears fishing in a stream, side-by-side.

"If we were a company, but not a coffee shop company, what kind of company would we be? Theo, you're next. This time, I'm going to change the pictures more quickly."

Theo gulped. Amy Ann yelled, "Go!"

Theo- Sporting event concessions!

Julia – Nanny services.

Theo stared at Julia. Amy Ann interjected, "Theo let me remind you and everyone else that we need to keep out comments, both negative and positive, to ourselves." She pointed to Daisy.

Daisy – Cookware…a special line of cooking clothes…for adventurous couples." She blushed.

Miles – Automotive repair to your door…and lawn maintenance too.

Smitty – Horse ranches with full amenities.

Georgia – Hot air balloon rides and circus rides.

G.Q. – Induction cooking stoves.

Anthony – Cheap adobe homes in all Green subdivisions: walk to every store – no cars.

Theo – Geothermal line of clothing that protects from heat and cold and wet, and looks like a normal suit or dress.

Daisy – Tours of South and Central America.

Miles – International business schools.

Smitty – Buy up 300 Dairy Queen franchises.

Amy Ann put up a new picture of a mermaid swimming alongside an underwater castle.

Georgia – Dance and martial arts schools for children.

G.Q. – Hydro culture coffee growers.

Anthony – Hotels – small, intimate hotels with living rooms with a communal eating area, but not a B&B – bigger and less personal.

At the end of the session, Amy Ann created a list of options for each question and they pledged to have another session around the three best for each question.

Question #1 and the three best options:

"How would the customer buy our product if we weren't in the store?"

1. Neighborhood and business area trucks.
2. Delivery with full breakfast or regular home/office delivery service like Netflix.

3. At bus stops and alternative fuel stations.

Question #2 and the three best options:
"If we weren't a coffee shop company, what sort of company would we be?"
1. Satellite Web services to Asia, Africa and Russia.
2. Green subdivisions, including stores and schools etc.
4. A community fostering hotel chain with shared eating and a large living room.

YOUR PERFECT STORM

Put together eight pictures that are detailed and colorful. At your next session hold a picture up every eight minutes.

Give each person a picture (possibly on a visual stimulation card) and ask him or her to write down 10 ideas while looking at the card.

Chapter 14

Mind mapping: Mind maps as Tools for Brainstorming

"Mind Maps are diagrams that work the way you think. They make it easy to understand, remember, and communicate complex information."

From www.novamind.com web site.

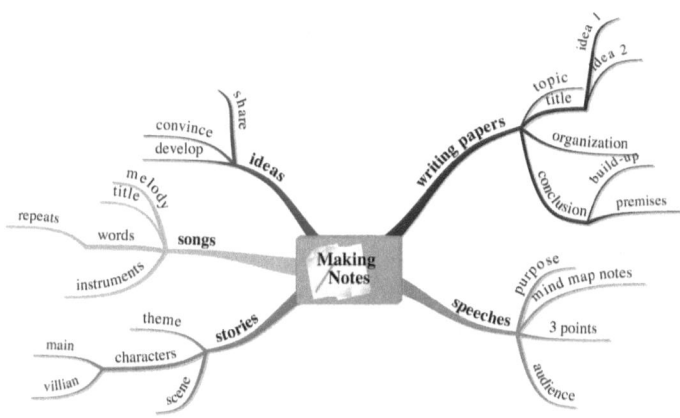

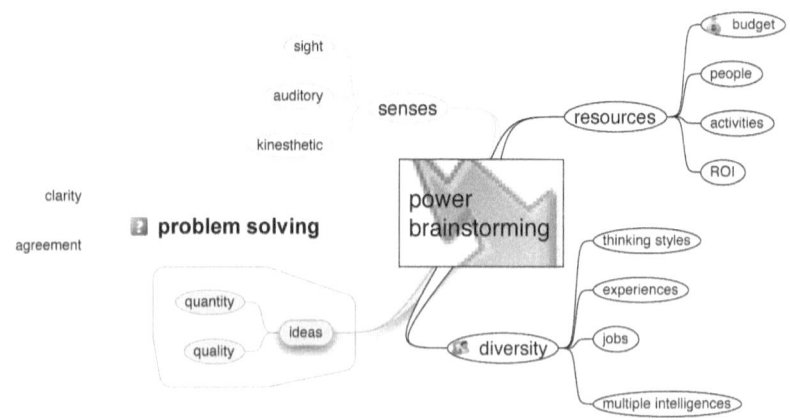

Mind mapping helps your memory and your brainstorming

As we have learned, a mind map is a physical drawing of how ideas are connected in our brain, thereby helping memory. Mind maps are also a way to use relationships of ideas and free association to bring out more ideas.

Our brain tries to organize subjects by relationships, and we extract pieces of memory the same way. Just think about how you might work on trying to remember a street name, for example. What most people say is that they look for associations in their "head" --people, places, or pictures they might connect to the name. So when you are studying a subject and you learn it using pictures, colors, keywords and points, and, most of all, relationships, you are helping your brain put it together in the most optimal way for remembering.

Also, you are using all the modes of learning at the same time. Each of us has one preferred learning mode – sight, hearing or kinesthetic (going through the physical motions). In doing mind maps we are using both sight and "doing," and if it is taking notes from a lecture or something we need to hear, we are using all three. In fact, you may have noticed that you sometimes say words out loud that you want to remember, as you write them down.

Mind maps are a way of "seeing" or showing the relationships of the ideas what we are attempting to understand. For those of us who subconsciously like our world to be more systematized, such as Safekeeping, Organized quadrant thinkers, mind maps help us organize ideas more systematically. For the Experimental, Big Picture quadrant thinkers you are not only able to use lots of pictures and colors, but the result is the "big picture."

Free Association

Start with your main topic or question at the center of a page. Draw 12 lines coming out from the center word and going around in a circle. Time yourself. Take 60 seconds to write one word on each of the 12 lines that comes to mind about the central word. If you are able to do this in a team, everyone starts with the same central word. No talking during the minute you are writing.

When you are finished, compare the 12 words each person wrote. How many are the same? It is unlikely that many of them will be the same. So you see how easy it is to come up with a dozen keywords, each related to the central word. If you have 10 people in the room you are likely to have almost 10 times 12 different words. The more people the more creativity. The more diversity in the areas mentioned in the Diversity chapter, the greater the differences in the lists and the greater the creativity.

Color and movement brings out creativity

When you physically draw you are using muscles and movement to express the ideas on paper or a board. It helps to be using more than one of your senses. It helps memory and creativity. Use colors to make the process and picture more interesting for your brain. That too helps memory and creativity.

A mind map is a powerful graphic technique that helps unlock your brain's potential. You work kinesthetically as you draw the map; you build visual memory as you look at what you have drawn; and you create connections in your brain between key ideas and words.

Mind mapping improves learning, as has been proven by thousands of students who improve test scores when they study by building a mind map of the study subject. The process of building a mind map of a subject or a chapter from a book forces you to think through the connections between the key point, keywords, and key ideas. Drawing the connections on paper helps imprint them in your brain. Once the subject is organized on a single page, you are often able to visualize the page while taking a test or explaining the subject to someone else.

If you have a mind map of your idea, proposal, or project and bring it with you to help you explain your idea to your manager, the executive committee, or a prospective customer, you will be able to explain much more clearly and succinctly. Your listeners will have the diagram to help them follow what you are saying. And, if appropriate, you can make copies of the mind map for your listeners to keep and refer to, as they explain your proposal or plan to the next person.

Mind mapping helps you think more clearly about a subject as you draw out the connections and make decisions about the keywords.

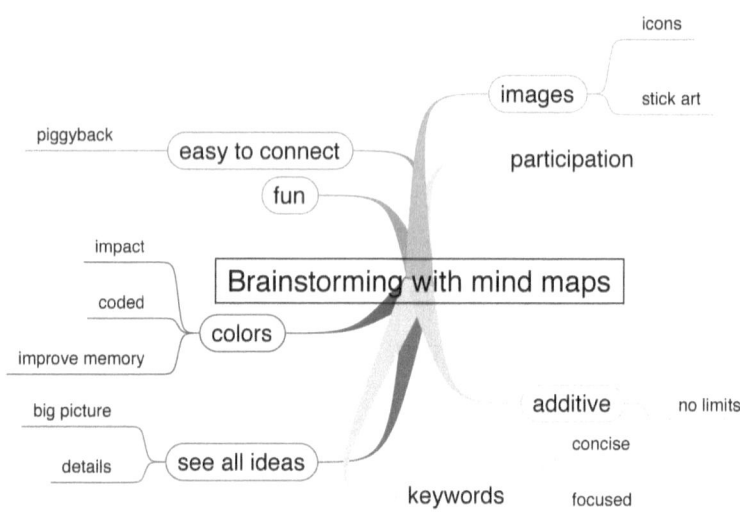

Here are ways that mind mapping helps you improve brainstorming and other thinking processes at work:

1. **Continuous Learning** is a requirement to move ahead in your career and for your company to be successful and grow. Learning is quicker and easier when the learner mind maps the subject, plus the learning lasts longer, recall is easier and more complete.
2. Get **Clarity** on a subject before you try to explain it to someone else. This can be done with something you are working on yourself at first, or it could be a team project that will have to be explained to others in the company. Building a mind map of only the keywords and how they relate to each other forces you to take the subject down to its essence.
3. **Explaining or selling your idea** to customers or internally requires your "presentation" to be concise and inspiring. Whether you are able to present your idea in person or have to put it in writing, it will be more convincing and show how well you have thought it out when you

have used mind maps as the organization tool. Even leaving a message for someone will be more concise and effective if you thought about what you wanted to say in a small mind map first. Think about times you got annoyed at a rambling voicemail.

4. *Giving a speech or presentation* to an audience can be made to sound natural, organized, and amazing when you only use one piece of paper with a mind map of the keywords (key points). What do you think to yourself when you sit in an audience and you see a speaker come to the lectern with a thick set of papers? One, "This will be long." Secondly, "He or she will read to us." Finally, "It will be boring."

5. *Taking notes* while in a meeting or presentation can be distracting as you try to write down everything you think you need in the standard sentence form. While you're trying to get the notes written, the speaker has gone on, and you may have missed something important. Worst of all you may have missed the joke and now are asking your laughing neighbors, "What did he say? What was that?" Instead when you get fairly proficient at taking notes using a mind map you will only write down the keywords and connect them with lines in ways that will help you reconstruct the parts you need later.

6. *Doing brainstorming with a team*, either in a face-to-face meeting or a net meeting or online. The many software tools now available let you share and work on a mind map using a computer and over the Internet. It is a way to document the brainstorm of ideas to either document and share later or share with the team immediately as all remotely look at screens or projected in a room. Seeing the visual of the different subheadings and directions helps everyone come up with even more ideas.

Mind mapping as an Exceptional Tool for Business

We've already talked about how mind mapping helps to brainstorm -- that it is a way to organize either brainstormed ideas, take notes during a presentation, plan a project, organize your thoughts before a speech, writing an important complex letter or article and a way to divide up a large brainstorming project to give pieces of it to smaller teams.

In addition, we have talked about its advantages in appealing to our various senses at the same time, especially visual and kinesthetic, to enhance our hearing memory, which is already involved in the teamwork of brainstorming.

Here is an example of a brainstorming mind map (made using Minjet's MindManager software) to explore ideas to improve customer service:

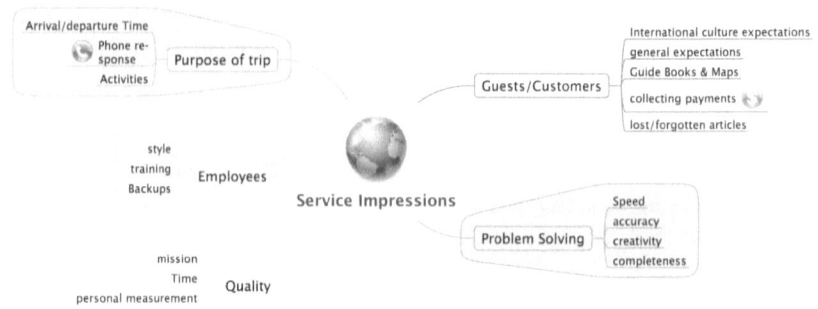

STORM SESSION 11

Here is a mind map that Amy Ann created from the session in the park:

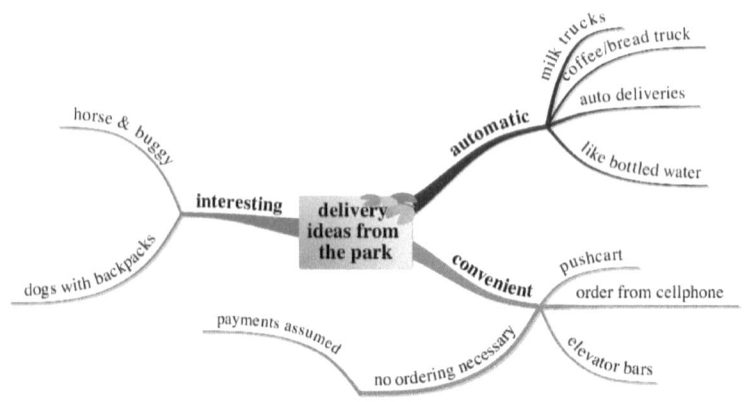

YOUR PERFECT STORM

Imagine a question and 10 final options coming from all the different thinking styles and intelligence types. It's time for you to create your own mind map.

Chapter 15

Clustering Explained

"To stay competitive, we have to lead the world in per-person creativity."

~ JIM CLIFTON, CEO, GALLUP ORGANIZATION
FROM THE ARTICLE: "THE ART OF WORK", FAST COMPANY,
AUGUST 2005, ISSUE 97 BY ANN MARSH

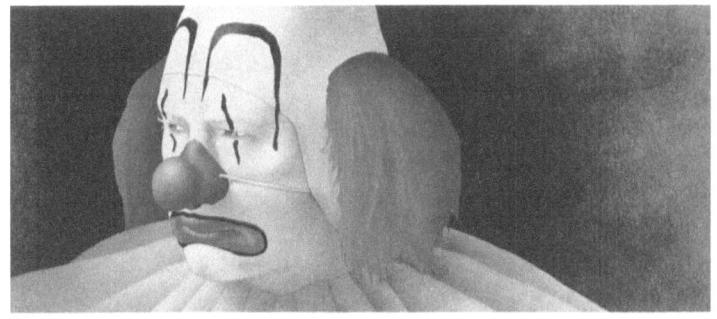

Jesters Do Often Prove Prophets
by Will Bullas, with permission of the artist. www.willbullas.com

Clustering is an activity that generates ideas, images and words without any attention to order. As you cluster, words and ideas can be thought of as "tumbling out." Clustering may be an individual or a group activity.

Sometimes the term *cluster diagrams* is mistakenly used to mean mind maps. The term *cluster* means to start by randomly writing down all the keyword ideas on a piece of paper, flip chart, or white board. When it appears as if there are plenty of keyword ideas or when it seems as if the flow is slowing down, you take a different color and start drawing lines (like a lasso) around the ideas that seem to fit together. Then for each cluster of keywords you come up with a single keyword or short phrase that could be a heading for that group.

For example, for the question: How can we restructure this department to eliminate an "us vs. them" attitude among the groups of workers? Here are some keywords:

- Flat
- Hierarchy
- Creative
- Space
- Games
- Manager
- Cubes
- Toys
- Meet
- Meetings
- Write
- Jokes
- Help
- Money
- New
- Informal
- Formal
- Ideas

Then, you would "lasso" related terms such as, *flat hierarchy* and *manager*, *toys* and *space* or *jokes* and *informal meetings*.

Working your keyword diagram by brainstorming randomly first can be a freer way of thinking about the topic or question as you first get started. For some groups or individuals this seems like a more natural brainstorming method.

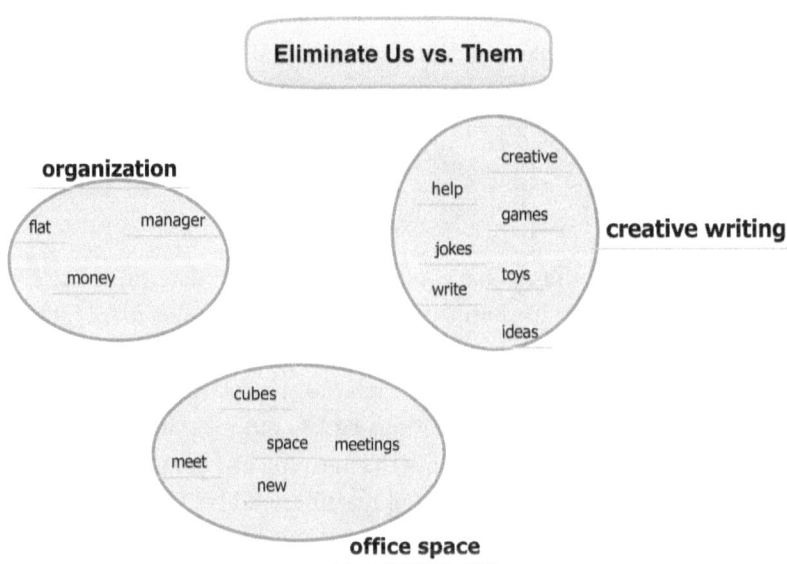

The clustering method was first named and described in books by Gabriel Rico. She has been evangelizing the topic and has written a number of books and articles that have influenced schools to adopt the method in their teaching. She advocates clustering, especially to teach and encourage writing skills.

The instructions are looser than for mind mapping. They are non-linear, even chaotic, allowing seemingly random variables into the picture. Clustering is a self-organizing process in which the mind-leaps going on can be made visible on a page.

Some school districts teach the clustering method. It is important that schools teach children some form of mind mapping or clustering since it improves a person's ability to organize their learning, improve their memory, study more efficiently, and write better.

My recommendation is that you try cluster diagrams sometimes and other times mind map out from a central concept or topic. You decide if one generally works better for you or works better in some situations. It is also an excellent way to vary the methods to keep your brainstorming sessions fresh and interesting, and most of all, productive.

Using a method like mind mapping or clustering helps you visualize your ideas and thinking.

The software programs available as of this writing are all listed in the Resource Section at the back of the book. All of them do a great job with mind mapping. ConceptDraw has an added feature that allows you to do free form brainstorming, ending up with clusters. Novamind lets you brainstorm with each branch and then have the software divide up the items into separate child branches.

 STORM SESSION 12

Julia had a firm walk; the walk, not of a soldier but of a determined pilgrim. Every day, she walked for 30 minutes on the woodland trail next to the building. On her walks, she tried to absorb her mind in what her eye fell upon: a splotch of sunlight, a tree frog, and a flower. Her job as a . . . was …a job. Julia had once enjoyed her work in telecommunications and found meaning in it. She still took satisfaction in a job well done, but the meaning had gone out of it for her. These recent turns in the brainstorming meetings had led her mind down its own "What if" path.

Always practical, Julia had asked herself to keep the bigger picture in mind. In other words, when thinking of career paths that she might enjoy. She considered that perhaps one of these would coincide with the company's new direction.

She made a mental note to mention to Amy Ann this new way into the same subject. Instead of thinking of new ventures for the company, think of new personal ventures and see where they might overlap.

For her part, Julia had already put herself through a rigorous individual brainstorming session.

Careful to think in all styles and to keep the different intelligences in mind, Julia had compiled this initial personal cluster.

Age: 57
Likes: Archery, carpentry, hiking.
Passions: radio, television and film
Goals: Generate excellent film documentaries and write a book.
Cluster keywords:

- Build

- Video
- Communications
- Voice
- Literature

From this cluster, Julia created this list of possible career options:

- Documentary filmmaker
- Journalist
- Corporate communications director
- Head of Developing Nations communications/media
- Facilitator in camp/seminar for leaders making policy choices/planning
- Famous author
- Movie director

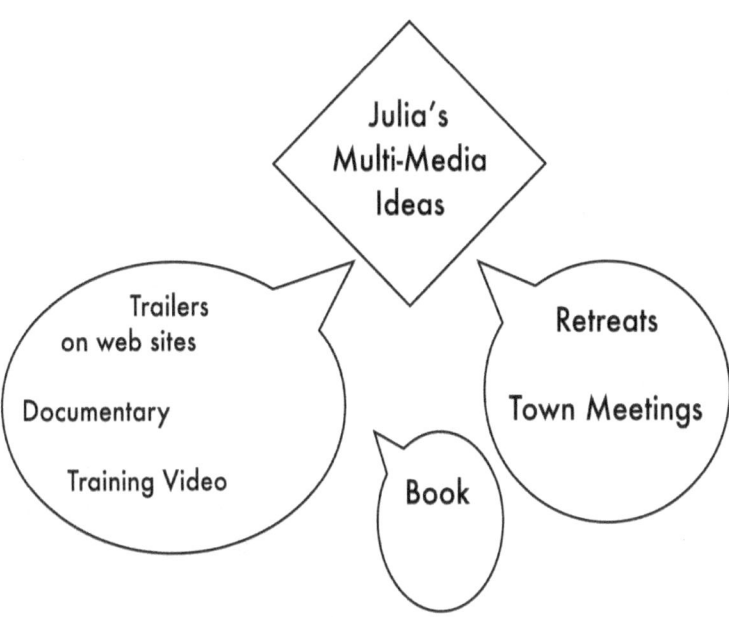

From this process, she created another cluster of possible ways to contribute to the company's goals sparked by her own interests.

- Shoot a documentary about a new franchise and the partners that decide to start it. Show it as a training video, also as an orientation.
- Make her book about how to reinvigorate a company's bottom line using employee innovation.
- Propose an initiative that calls for town meeting style retreats at sites that allow for a large number of franchise owners to join with corporate decision-makers in giving open feedback. Create a video of this interaction and ask to have the role of Facilitator.
- Post trailers online at the company Web site and have links on related sites such as "How to Operate a Franchise" and various small business sites.
- Develop a reputation as a creator of dynamic photography and a documenter.

From this cluster, Julia knew that she had created the kernels she needed to eventually transform her job into something exciting once more.

"Ha!" Julia let out a laugh. "Stick to one road at a time, Julia." She knew her tendency to jump from possibility to possibility, instead of thoroughly exploring each one.

Walking back to her desk, she passed Miles and G.Q. starting out for the trail. They were laughing and talking excitedly. To see the former staunch opponents so buddy-buddy, took Julia for a start.

"Julia, quit staring!" G.Q. called, his gray crew cut bobbing along happily next to Mile's youthful black head.

She smiled and shrugged her shoulders. Brainstorming together had finally broken those two down.

At the next full group brainstorming session, as they were continuing to explore ways to bring greater media exposure to the brand, Julia's mind was immersed in thoughts of film methods, balancing voice and viewpoint and file editing methods. She was surprised at the beginning of the session as if on cue, to hear Miles and G.Q.'s voices ring out in unison, "Pool Halls!"

The entire session was infused with a strange, almost hilarious energy as people truly had a sense of being on the edge of creating something new and big.

At the end of the session, the final company brainstorming cluster for media expansion looked like this:

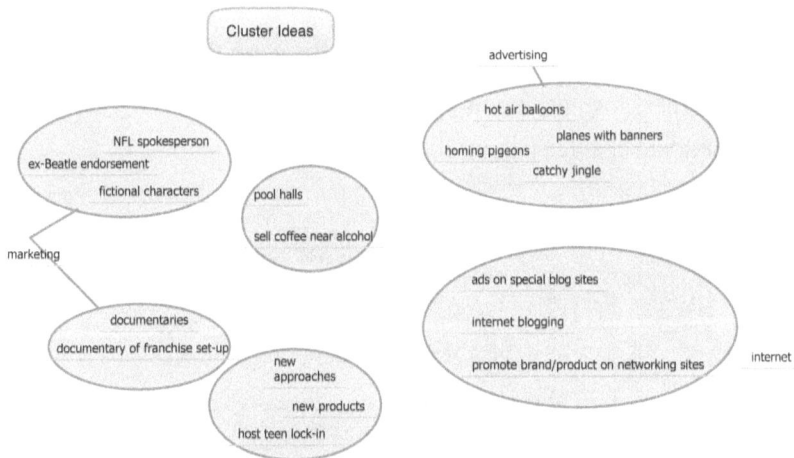

And then the clustered ideas were used to make a mind map which could be used to brainstorm further.

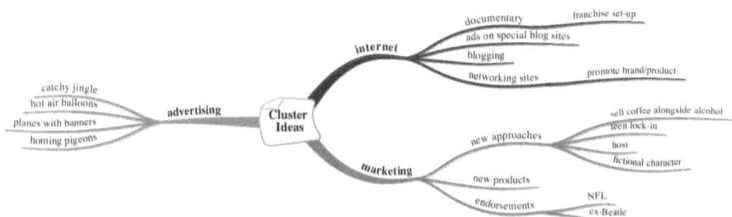

- Pool Halls with wide screen TVs. Selling coffee products alongside alcohol.
- Documentary of the franchise set-up process
- Hot air balloons
- Planes with banners
- Homing pigeons with messages
- NFL spokesperson
- Ex-Beatle endorsement

- Host teen lock-in for Halloween and make it reality TV
- Articles in newspapers about new approaches and products
- Radio ads with truly catchy jingles that you can't forget –
- Radio shows with comics always joking about the brand and products
- Internet blogging, ads on special blog sites
- Fictional character to promote brand and product on all networking sites.

YOUR PERFECT STORM

What would you do if you wanted to re-invigorate your job from the inside out, without actually changing jobs?

What would you suggest that your company do if it had to create a new product or service or both?

How would you tie these two together for mutual benefit?

CHAPTER 16

THE FOREST, THE TREES AND THE FLOWER

Take the time to separately consider a subject or question from a distance, looking at the whole forest, and then close up, examining the individual trees.

© Cindy Hughes - Fotolia.com

Take your topic that you want to brainstorm and start up two mind maps, one that is a forest (big picture) mind map and one that is a trees (detailed picture) mind map. You can also use one of the other brainstorming techniques described in this book doing it twice, one thinking forest, the other focusing on the trees.

The Forest:

During a forest brainstorming you ask questions and explore options by looking at the big picture rather than any details. What will be the results? How will others view the project? What will it look or feel like when it is finished? Where will the project lead? How big can it get? How big should it get? It is a macro approach.

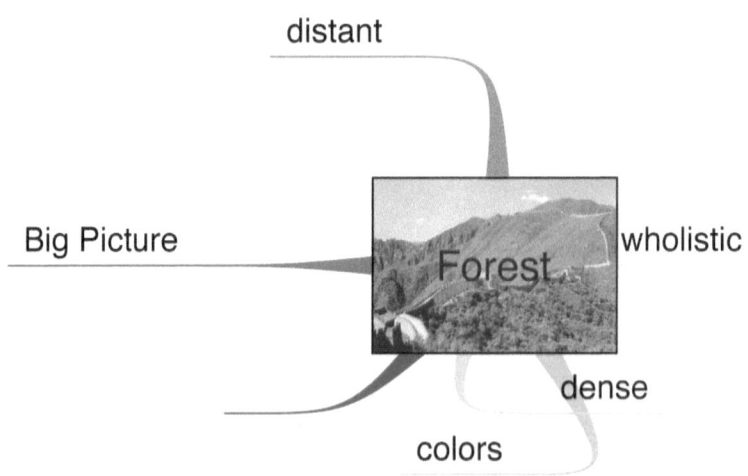

The Trees:

What needs to be in the detailed plan? What are the attributes of the parts needed? Who or what skills are needed? What supplies will help the project? This then becomes the micro approach.

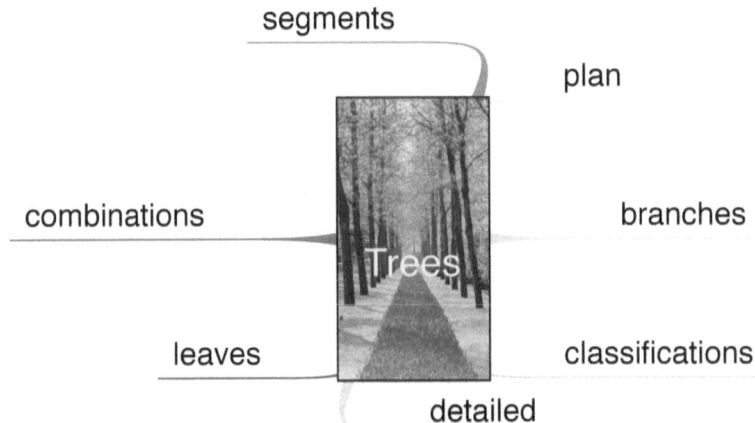

Lotus blossom Method

The Flower or the Lotus Blossom is a tool that combines structure with unstructured brainstorming.

Write the problem or issue you are brainstorming in the center square (use a large sheet of paper, flipchart or whiteboard, if possible). Write down the first eight ideas in each of the squares surrounding the central square. Take each of the eight ideas and write them in the square with the same color/letter and then brainstorm each one separately, coming up with eight ideas for each of the surrounding squares. You can keep expanding the lotus blossom as many times as you have time, using the same format.

Go ahead and write in the third-tier boxes below detailed ideas related to the more general concepts, such as "energy use" or "legal structure (taxes)" etc.

Lotus blossom

		F			C		G	
				F	C	G		
				Staff	Skills	Legal issues		
	B			B	Reduce factory costs	D		D
				Leases		Energy use		
				E	A	H		
				Materials	Process	Purchas-ing		
		E			A		H	

2

 STORM SESSION 13

Fourteen days after the first meeting, an email from Madeline, the company CFO, arrived in Amy Ann's inbox. It read: "Amy Ann, will you please distribute the following links and articles to your team in anticipation of the next meeting?"

Amy Ann's eyebrows shot up as she inspected the files. Demographic tendencies in media use, especially media use by mothers, Boomers born before 1956 and Gen X overall. Rifling through the options from the previous session, she saw "Advertising with text messages, promoting brand through blogs and radio shows." Shaking her head curiously, she looked up to see Miles standing at her cubicle entrance.

"Oh, Hi Miles."

"Hi."

She sat looking at him for a minute or two. She raised her eyebrows and smiled quizzically. Miles cleared his throat.

"Amy Ann, I'm going out for a turn around the trail. Would you like to come with me?"

Amy Ann laughed, "Sure! I thought you had a problem or something. Let's go." They walked out together and were quickly spotted with bits of sunlight coming through the tall birch trees. Amy Ann was in a good mood. She was practically skipping, in fact.

"You seem buoyant," Miles remarked.

"I am. I'm buoyant."

"Any special reason?"

"No. Not really. I'm just enjoying the work I'm doing and feeling like it's a new phase of my life."

Miles cleared his throat again. "Amy Ann, is there someone special you're seeing right now?"

"No. Not at all. I don't date that much. Why?"

"Well, you can probably guess why. I'd like to ask you out."

Amy Ann stopped and looked into Miles' eyes. "Miles, if we didn't work together…"

"You have a strict policy on that?"

"Yes, very." She touched his arm lightly, "I like you, you know."

Miles blushed. "Oh. Um. Great. Well, if you'll excuse me, I have a resignation to tender."

"You're kidding!"

"Yes. I am, for now, anyway," he laughed lightly and changed the subject to the upcoming holidays. The two eventually parted at the door laughing at a joke about Colorado hunters and snowboarders.

Once back at her desk, Amy Ann broadcasted the information Madeline had sent out to the team. The next meeting was scheduled to occur in six days. Amy Ann began to dig into studies on media use, buying habits and success rates for celebrity-endorsed products; in particular what sorts of celebrities and what groups responded best to them. She knew that once Suzanne Sommers had come out about bio-identical hormones, she had urged her mother to take that path, and when Lucy Liu raved about Eucerin™ as a natural moisturizer, she had bought a tube the next day.

On the day of the session, Amy Ann stood before the group in the Rice Crispy Treat Room. She was wearing a white dress with turquoise and red accents.

The group came in all at once, talking loudly among themselves. Everyone: G.Q., Anthony, Miles, Julia, Smitty, Georgia and Daisy were milling around in the room excitedly.

Amy Ann made a note that extensive information sent out in advance created premature discussions that were hard to capture.

"People! Team!" Amy Ann raised her hands over her head in supplication. Please take a seat and please save your ideas until they can be properly documented. Or better yet, have you been keeping good notes?" Everyone obediently took a seat.

"Let's not waste any time," Amy Ann proposed, grabbing a marker. "Each easel represents a specific 'branch' of the mind map that we are working with. First of all, we will talk about the 'forest' or those ideas that are high level and general. Secondly, we will drill down to the 'trees' so-to-speak."

"Right now, I'm going to ask you a question and based on the information you received a week ago, please respond, going counter-clockwise. I'm going to count on you to keep up the pace. We want content-rich answers. They don't have to be presented quickly, but that would be good." She looked at the now well-oiled brainstorming team with pride, as they sat poised like long-distance runners. "My team," Amy Ann thought. "Here is the question." She pulled a mask off the projection screen,

"How should we revitalize our brand using these elements: music, celebrity, Internet and radio? Please note that we want a message that keeps that sort-of family and friends feeling, but maybe takes on a modern, energetic edge. Think about:

1. What will be the results?
2. How will others view what we are doing?
3. What will it look and feel like?
4. Where will the project lead?
5. How big will it get?

6. How big should it get?"

Julia started right out of the gate, "A video documenting two different sets of partners as they start up their franchise, like the reality shows. We get to see their lives and feel connected to them. We watch them develop the business and listen to their feedback facing the camera. When it's all done, we use the documentary in orientation and to recruit new franchisees."

Amy Ann tried to interrupt, but Julia plunged ahead, like a river after a rain. "This could be a project that was continued each year, so that there were archives. Eventually, once upper-management got the hang of it, we would video them brainstorming together, after watching the videos, and then coming up with changes in store and brand policy as a result. This is the kind of 'opening up' that studies show Gen X likes to see in the workplace. It's not a flattening of hierarchy, but it's a greater level of communication that can only help the overall corporate culture." She paused and said no more.

"OK," Amy Ann stopped writing on the easel. "That was an example of the forest and a few trees. Those details, like what Gen X likes to see in the workplace, are what we will be looking for in the next phase. Let's write it down for the next stage and, let's move on!"

Smitty began speaking slowly, "You're going to need to bring music into this in a big way. I know from the literature we received that the 50 and 65-year-olds aren't too keen on downloading music, but I guarantee you that there is a huge group of coffee drinkers out there who never go anywhere without plugs in their ears. So, I suggest a bridge between the really catchy jingles and comedic dialogue on the radio and more popular songs sung by celebrities who endorse us. For instance, Sting or Bono or Ravi Shankar coming together for a jam session, with our brand/logo as a sponsor. This would be a set that was only available from our Web site or if you plugged in a code found on the bottom of a cup to the browser on your cell phone."

Daisy picked up quickly, "A newspaper ad with a celebrity associated with clean living, like Darrel Hannah talking about how she can rely on our company's integrity in terms of organic growing, non-sewage watering and fair labor practices."

G.Q. added, "I think a nice big picture, spread across the wall of a pool hall of a beautiful woman lounging in a leather chair, drinking a cup of coffee that says, 'This is where I like to hang out and meet new people.' I think that is the best ad of all."

Anthony continued with the idea, "Adding the option of juice smoothies and even wheat grass would be a huge pull for every demographic. No offence, but some people want a little raw food with their syrupy stuff."

Georgia said, "What about taking the rock star endorsements all the way and hosting a huge concert with our products as concessions. We could then sell the CDs in our stores, and maybe Julia could shoot a documentary of the concert, with Boomers who had been to other great concerts talking about their experiences and the differences….almost like we're weaving ourselves into the social fabric."

Julia jumped in, "Cool! We need to recruit some top bloggers."

All eyes were now in Miles, who was standing against the giant mural of a rice crispy treat, his hands in his pockets. "Community…community connection…media. What about offering full-fledged syndication and endorsement to a blogger who can prove through first-hand experience that our stores are more than just coffee shops, they are community stop-gaps? I mean talk about the *meaning* behind one of our coffee shops? I'm talking business, romance, conflict negotiation and parenting support."

Amy Ann, busy labeling ideas "forest" and "tree," finally looked up. "What about TV?"

Georgia shot out, "TV is only heavily watched in the Gen Y group, though all groups watch it to some extent. Boomers aren't big on cable or high definition TV."

Daisy said, "I think some TV presence would be good, like TV ads for the concert and maybe shots of a fictional character from the social networking sites so that we can create a connection between the photo of the person on MySpace.com. I mean, make them more three-dimensional. A lot of college kids watch TV sporadically, but go to their social networking sites religiously."

"OK," Amy Ann called out, "What is the new tone, the new look and feel? List them all." She pointed to Julia.

"I like the World look and feel, a mix of Sting and Ravi Shankar. A little Cuban mamba and some Dijavan from Brazil. Maybe a coffee drink that has some exotic spice in it."

Smitty said simply, "Down home country with green Earth."

Anthony said, "I like a sharper image type look and feel, maybe a whoosh sound, some wind and a feeling like you're in an inner world."

Georgia said, "To my mind, the look and feel should be like what we have now, which is friends and family, but a little more edgy. I would say show friends of diverse backgrounds with some melody, then drumming and laughing then back to the melody; and keep the fire, but put it outside."

Daisy said, "Well, I like a plain but classic feel. One or two people just talking simply without scripts, maybe being funny, and always have different people. It would take a keen eye, but would appeal to everyone and appear less canned...No offense to any of your suggestions!"

Amy Ann asked, "Does it stay the same or change over time?"

"Hey," Miles interrupted her, "I didn't get to offer my look and feel: Hogs on the road, the feel of the wind in your face, horses charging through the snow, and then cut to sudden silence showing someone curled up with earphones or a book and a cup of coffee. Contrast, people. That's what it's all about!"

G.Q. spoke up, "OK. I think that it should start out simple, and then as we get feedback and try new things, evolve to a look and feel and sound that is incredibly contagious and identifiable...part of pool halls everywhere."

An hour passed as the group completed the forest portion of the question and added many ideas into the tree section. Amy Ann stopped writing. "We're out of time. A lot of the ideas you gave actually fit into the tree portion." Amy Ann passed out bottles of vitamin water and thin mint Girl Scout cookies.

"I'll work up these ideas into mind maps and send them out to you. Next time we'll answer these questions: 'What would we do with this idea if money were no object? Who would we partner with if we could partner with anyone? How can we make money on lifestyle offerings rather than product changes?'"

Miles stretched his hands over his head, happily. "I feel so important."

"Yes," Smitty agreed, tapping his boot rhythmically. It's like being king of the world to think of all these ideas."

Julia injected, "Or queen."

G.Q. noted, "Remember, power corrupts." He smiled mischievously. Amy Ann realized that it was the first time she'd seem him smile.

YOUR PERFECT STORM

JJ Pentworth Department Store sells vendor clothing and products as well as their own clothing brand. The store has been losing money, and they've decided, after doing market research, to drop their own brand, stop selling clothing and shoes and focus exclusively on selling specialized building supplies wholesale. By compiling large orders for environmentally friendly products, their builder buyers will be able to purchase these at rates comparable to regular chemically treated or less-efficient products.

Ask your group to brainstorm on these questions:

"How can we deconstruct the JJ Pentworth operation efficiently and humanely?"

Create a forest.

Create a tree or trees.

Take one aspect/idea from the forest and use it in a Lotus diagram.

Chapter 17

Brainstorming Card Decks

"You should look for all the evidence that goes against your view."

—JAMES MONTIER, STRATEGIST, DRESDNER KLEINWORT WASSERSTEIN IN FAST COMPANY MAGAZINE, FASTCOMPANY.COM

Fridays after Five
by Will Bullas, with permission of the artist. www.willbullas.com

There are a number of card decks developed specifically to accelerate brainstorming. Thinkpak® by Michael Michalko, the Creative and Innovative Whack Packs® by Roger von Oech, and KnowBrainer® from SolutionPeople® to name three well-known ones.

Each of these card deck tools allows you to either brainstorm as an individual or to break into small groups to tackle separate problems or the same question through different perspectives. In my experience, having a number of intensive groups all working on the same question(s) brings in valuable variety. A valuable aspect of the card decks is that they require the brainstormer to continue with the idea and elaborate and expand upon it. This is a "deeper" process than simply spitting out thoughts in a chain. The drawback is that the brainstormer might censor his or her own ideas because they are not in a timed interval. This is why I suggest that when two or more people work together, one can hold the cards and keep time; that is, keep the other person(s) responding at a fairly fast pace.

The KnowBrainer® is a set of cards attached with a rivet so that you can't lose any, and also because they are meant to be used in order. At each point in the innovation brainstorming process, there are specific cards to accelerate the process: 1. Investigate, 2. Create, 3. Evaluate, and 4. Activate. Each section has question cards to invigorate your thinking, picture cards to inspire, quote cards to cause you to stop and think more deeply, and keywords to spark more ideas. Examples of one question from each of the four steps:

1. How should success look, feel and sound?
2. If the sky is the limit, what might be possible?
3. What could be the full potential investment?
4. Who must be sold or persuaded?

Thinkpak™ from Michael Michalko

Go through the cards one at a time and expand ideas completely with each card before going to the next. As with the other decks of cards, they can be used when you need some prompting tools and are working on your own or with a group.

Whack Packs™ from Roger von Oech are hand-held tools that use questions, key words, quotes and images to stimulate thinking and ideas.

The Creative Whack Pack™ and Roger Van Oech's newer set, called the Innovative Whack Pack™, work well in a group or for you to use on your own. The pictures add a lot of humor to brainstorming. I sometimes shuffle and pass out a certain number to each person. Then we each take turns reading one and leading the group in idea generation. You can also pick a card at random and work on its subject until you feel you need a new one.

 STORM SESSION 14

"I want you to partner with the person sitting next to you, move to a corner, and once you are ready I will announce the question." Amy Ann stood in the center of the Fanning Birch Middle School Gym. She was wearing a workout suit and had a whistle around her neck.

Julia raised her hand, "May I ask, where are we going to sit?"

"I have placed tumbling mats on the floor for you to sit cross-legged, or if you prefer, you can sit in the bleachers." Amy Ann pointed to the old wooden bleachers, lovingly scared with penknife declarations of love.

Smitty and Miles moved to sit on mats under the west basketball hoop.

Daisy and Anthony settled down by the equipment bins. Julia and G.Q. took their places on the bleachers, and Amy Ann gave Georgia permission to work by herself, which she preferred.

"The question, Amy Ann said calmly, "is here." She pointed to the scoreboard, which displayed the question in green neon:

"How can we actually involve our customers in creating our new brand, so that the process uses media and stays effective to all demographic groups?"

"You have 30 minutes per person. I expect you to just focus on this one overall goal: Create lots of ideas. The reason is that we've done a lot of investigation into media use and buyers and we aren't ready to evaluate ideas yet.

Remember, people, we want to get out of the box, big time here. I don't want you to rest on typical practices or tradition. Be freaky, be way out, be radical and get me some ideas like nobody has ever had before!" Amy Ann enjoyed playing the role of coach very much. "Go!" She blew her silver whistle.

Smitty handled his visual stimulation cards with the ease of an old shark. He handed the first card to Miles. It was a picture of a molecule of cow manure combusting and producing energy. The colors were phantasmal, and the men found themselves momentarily entranced in the enlarged world of decay and rebirth. "Focus, man!" Smitty prodded him. "How are we going to get Joe and Lisa Average on board with helping us create a new look and feel? What's in it for them?" Smitty smiled.

Miles looked at the picture and then started talking, as Smitty took notes in his small spiral pad.

"OK, I'm thinking first of all that this guy, this person -- because it could be a woman, this person would need to have a connection a real personal connection to contributing. Let's see. If they're into blogging and videos and music, then I guess it's just a matter of motivating them. If they're really not, then, we've got to bring them in at a different level. I'm thinking about my mom and dad. They don't really watch much TV, just movies from Netflix. Also, they like to get together with friends in person. One thing though, they really like listening to audio books while they drive long distances. They also like to listen to humorous radio shows. I think that that group would be interested in winning a trip for two to another country if they can create an audio diary of funny/touching events. These wouldn't necessarily have to be directly connected to the product or stores, just sponsored by them. Also, we could have one of those on-air talk shows where people can be the host of it and have whatever guest they want, as long as they can tell a personal story that involves our store or brand or product in some way. This way, older Boomers could get what they want – a trip, and they could participate in the kind of friendly conversation, antidotal entertainment that they like."

"I'm thinking 'block parties,' he continued, "but held in the stores for certain neighborhoods and having them post photos of the party online and send them out to their friends."

Smitty, licked his pencil and kept writing, his big hands, surprisingly agile.

Amy Ann called out, "Stop! Switch!"

Next to the equipment bins, Daisy handed Anthony her pale blue Apple laptop, and he opened a new Word file, saving it as "DaisyGymSession.doc."

"I can type 50 words a minute, so give it your best shot," he said with a smile, his heart still pounding at the idea of a wilderness weekend, documented for YouTube.com with high mountain passes and cave explorations then a hot cup of coffee, and firelight cameos of the day, and closing with an edgy ballad.

Anthony handed Daisy a card. "This is for you, My Dear." Daisy saw the aerial view of a beach, each square inch covered with bright umbrellas, the tips of toes and elbows showing and strips of burning sand.

"Go!" Amy Ann shouted and blew her shiny whistle.

"I like your idea of an edgy ballad, but I would add that there is a competition among bands to come up with the ballad that will get air play. Then, every other year, we host another battle of the bands and songwriters. In addition, we need art galley style contests with the stores filled with submissions and videos too that people can watch in the stores. The store customers can vote in person or online, and then the store employees and executives get to weigh in too. It's like *American Idol*."

Daisy paused and looked again at the umbrellas. "Some people will not want to interact in any way. Some people, like mothers with children, might fall through the cracks and that is why".... she looked up at the old ceiling and seemed to hear the voices of all the children echoing in the big room. "That is why, the company will go to them, to their blog sites and their social networking sites and talk about what they might get out of participation, greater access to a supportive community...no, that's not enough. I think what they should get is some sort of tutoring services for their child or children, when they are school age. I think they would really put their heart and soul into it to get their kids a head start academically. Also….I like the idea of an online TV show. I like to watch TV online, since I don't have a TV. If we could have professional actors in a coffee shop setting and pay the going rate for scripts from our customers, I think a lot of people would jump at the chance, creatively and monetarily."

Stop! Amy Ann blew her whistle.

"Please stand up and stretch." Miles noticed that Amy Ann was bouncing a basketball. "It's time for Georgia and G.Q. to pick their teams. We're going to play a little one on one!"

Georgia, a die-hard basketball fan, shot to the center of the court and said, "I pick Amy Ann!"

G.Q., not to be pre-empted, ran to the highest bleacher, raised his fist and yelled, "I call Julia!" Everyone except Miles looked at him blankly. This was not the pick they would have expected, but Miles knew what G.Q. knew, that Julia had gone to college on a basketball scholarship and still played once a week with her 14 nieces. For Julia, basketball was a family affair.

Miles laughed and joined G.Q.'s team on his own. Anthony walked over to Georgia's team, and Daisy volunteered to act as referee. G.Q. and Georgia shot for first throw, and Georgia got it. The game was played with silent intensity. Julia, acting as forward, took the ball 10 times in that many minutes, making every shot. Amy Ann and Miles managed to dribble down the court and set up three shots before the game ended after half an hour. Daisy blew the plastic whistle Amy Ann had given her. " I declare G.Q.'s team the winner, but both teams get the prize, which is…" she paused mischievously, "free coffee!"

The teams groaned good-naturedly and tossed the ball at Daisy, before they all returned to their cars and, eventually, their cubes in the office building three miles away. Alone in the gym, Amy Ann shot a few baskets, tucked her clipboard under her arm, put her whistle in her pocket and turned off the lights before leaving.

YOUR PERFECT STORM

A large hotel chain, based in Dallas, Texas, owns the Hotel Blanca Bonito on the Yucatan Peninsula. A recent hurricane has demolished the structures around the hotel and left its beach littered with debris. The hotel itself, however, escaped any real damage. It had been booked for a string of high profile weddings and large conventions worth millions in revenue.

What can the Hotel Blanc Bonito do to maintain its engagements and contribute to the recovery of the neighboring businesses, without losing money?

Use a set of cards and break into teams of four. Each person in the group takes on one of these aspects of the question:

(1) Investigate, (2) Create, (3) Evaluate, and (4) Activate

Take 30 minutes per person with the person to the right taking notes.

Books with Exercises

There are so many wonderful books with exercises that you can use for on your own brainstorming or in a group.

Here are some of my favorites, but I would appreciate it if you, my wonderful reader, would send me the reference information for any you have found to be helpful that I have not mentioned.

Michael Michalko has written spectacular books: *Thinkertoys: A Handbook of Creative-Thinking Techniques (2nd Edition); Cracking Creativity: The Secrets of Creative Genius.*

Tony Buzan's *The Mind Map Book* is the best first book on the topic of mind mapping because it gives you all the ideas and tools necessary to get you started and explains why the technique works so well. Buzan has written many books, some of them are repetitious, but find the ones that fit your needs best. If you have children, I recommend his book, *Mind Mapping for Kids*. The examples in the book are British. If you do not live in Great Britain, you can help your children by choosing examples from their own schoolwork and accomplish the same thing. You will do any child a favor and help them do better in school if you take the time to work through that book with them. You may also learn more about mind mapping for yourself in the process.

Michael Gelb's books *Think like Leonardo daVinci* and *Discover your Genius*. These are excellent books both for learning how to enhance your idea-generation and for exercises you can do on your own or with a group.

For additional resources see the Resources Section.

Chapter 18

Brainstorming With A Large Audience

It is better to know some of the questions than all of the answers.

JAMES THURBER
US AUTHOR, CARTOONIST, HUMORIST, &
SATIRIST (1894 - 1961)

© *Stephen Coburn fotolia*

Brainstorming with a large group requires techniques designed to make everyone feel that they are part of the process, collect individual ideas, and allow them to share those ideas as quickly as possible with the whole group.

I have found that making laptop computers part of the process works well in large groups.

You can either put each person on his or her own computer, or have one person designated to capture ideas on the computer. Tell everyone not to be concerned with spelling and grammar and to type as fast as they can. Quantity is more important than quality for the first round.

If laptops are not available, pass out handouts with the question(s) and guidelines for brain writing, word chaining, and/or individual mind maps. In addition, include blank sheets in the handouts for people to record their ideas per each technique, then have everyone sign their sheets and hand them in to generate pride in their contributions.

Staff members or volunteers can combine all the results. Announce the number of ideas generated and combine them into one large mind map or a list by categories.

Follow-Up

Follow-up an original large group brainstorming session by starting where you left off and by sharing the results and categories of ideas from the previous session. Then you have a number of options:

> Option 1: If you have enough participants, divide the categories and give each small team one of the categories to brainstorm further. Give them open-ended questions related to the category to get their creative juices flowing.
>
> Option 2: If the group is not large enough to divide up or the space isn't conducive to breakouts, choose one category at a time and explore and brainstorm first to generate open-ended questions for that category.
>
> Then start brainstorming the category further by exploring each of the open-ended questions. If something comes up that fits one of the other categories, put a star next to it to be added later to that other category.
>
> Option 3: Share the prior results, explaining that it is just the beginning. Start with some on-your-own brainstorming first and then

bring all the ideas together by clustering or mind mapping with ideas from the previous session; and keep right on generating more ideas.

Remote Brainstorming Online

It is more difficult but not impossible to brainstorm with a team of people who are not in the same location.

If possible, schedule a Web conference. Pass the input control around, so each has it for five minutes or some specified time during which they ask open-ended questions related to the subject, while everyone else submits ideas.

If you need to work remotely and not at the same time, start an online mind map using one of the mind mapping software programs and open it up for additions from all participants. Reorganize the ideas as needed, but not until there are plenty there. The ideas will flow more quickly if they don't spend much time thinking about where it goes in the map.

Use a mind mapping program that the entire team has learned how to use and add items as they occur instead of waiting till someone else gets around to typing them.

Brainstorming Connected to an Activity or Observation

What if you need to observe customers using your product or service or to try something out yourself as part of the brainstorming?

This is an excellent opportunity to catch all the ideas as they occur. Use recording devices, if speaking out loud will not disturb the process or inhibit others from coming up with their own ideas.

Otherwise, have forms or blank mind maps or just pads of paper ready. Emphasize the importance of getting every idea written down before it has any chance of being forgotten or overruled in by one's own mind.

Advanced Brainstorming Techniques

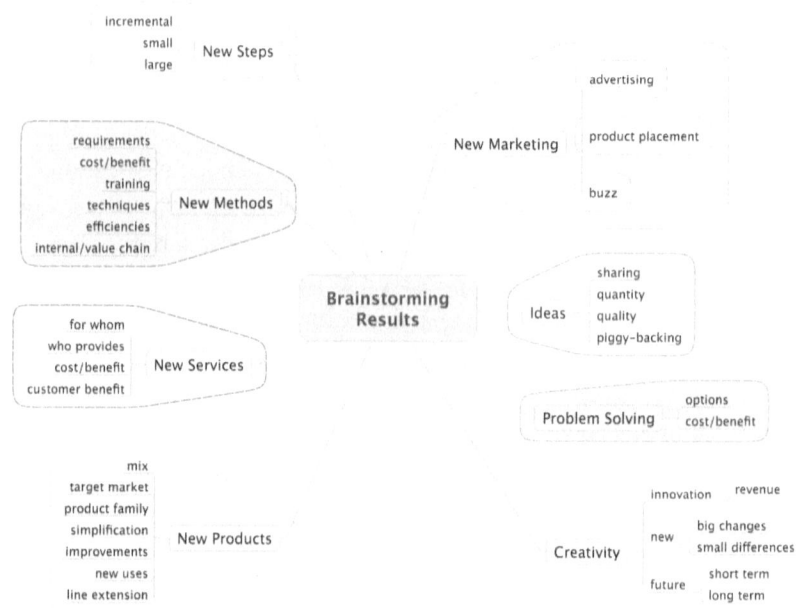

 STORM SESSION 15

The group of 30 people filed into the darkened meeting hall one-by-one. All around them orange lamps hung from the ceiling, casting a firelight glow. Over each laptop computer at the round tables hung one of the cone-shaped orange lamps, making the tables seem almost theatrical or surgical.

As everyone took a seat at the six tables, Amy Ann made her way to the front of the room. She pushed a button on her remote control, and an image flashed on the large screen behind her.

It was a picture of the San Francisco Bridge at sunset.

Perhaps it was the semi-darkness, perhaps it was anticipation, but no one in the room was talking.

"Thank you all for coming," Amy Ann began. "Besides our usual group of seven, I have also invited key people from Accounting, Operations and Marketing. As you know, the last time we met, in the gym, we brainstormed on media campaign ideas. Well, now the company has decided to move forward with an Internet/video campaign, a radio campaign and a newspaper campaign. The estimated cost for this level of marketing/advertising will be 25 million. We expect that these campaigns will inject a much needed shot of franchise investors, as well as patronage and other types of investors."

"We have 10 million to spend, so the question is: How can we modify operations to free up the additional 15 million that we need?"

"To remind you all, here is a basic breakdown of our asset structure." Another image appeared on the screen, this one a chart of entities showing the cash flow process. I know that you have all received this information three days ago and have had time to familiarize yourself with it.

"As you can see, we have 40,000 stores worldwide. We receive five percent of revenue from those stores. We sell 25 licenses a month at 1.5 million each. Here are our overhead costs broken down, our investments, stock price and shares held. You can see from this pie chart, that we are running a tight ship, yet license sales have gradually fallen in the last five years. We are now selling 20 licenses a month only. Our revenue share from existing stores has fallen 20 percent from 3.3 million a month to 2.6 million over a seven- year period."

Nine years ago the company put a prepared plan in place to deal with this drop, and we are not experiencing a crisis here. As those who work in Accounting know, we had measures ready at the sign of a one percent drop almost a decade ago, so these losses are under control and have been for some time. The company is stable. In fact, that is why we are broaching this subject now. Management has decided to use the media ideas the brainstorming group generated to re-grow the company in the next five to seven years. To do that, we want to generate extra revenue for advertising.

While we've asked hard questions and made hard decisions over the last seven years, we still need to ask more questions and make more decisions if we want to really grow and transform in new ways. So:

"What do we need to cut? What do we need to restructure? What can we add or subtract to create a cushion for advertising on a large scale over a 12-month period?"

Please type your responses into a blank email and send it to me. My helpers will combine all of your answers into one list that we can look at together on the screen. You have seven minutes. Go!"

Without further ado, Amy Ann walked to the back of the room and sat quietly under a shining orange, glass dome.

Their lips pressed tightly together, their faces pinched in concentration, the eerie faces of the 30 employees peering into their screens evoked miners searching for gold, which indeed they were.

After seven minutes of the clatter of keyboard keys and nothing else, Amy Ann walked back to the front of the room. "Please stop." The orange lights abruptly shut off, and the room for two seconds was left with only the laptops for luminescence. Then the main lights burst on in blinding whiteness, and everyone looked at everyone else almost shyly.

"While we compile these results, please feel free to walk around. You will find coffee and gluten-free brownies, as well as over-the-top pound cake on each side of the room. If you'd like to do some aerobics, Cecil is leading a 15-minute stretch and jog class next door."

Immediately, the low rumble of human voices became a beehive of conversation and activity.

At the end of fifteen minutes, Amy Ann waved her hands wildly and motioned to everyone to take a seat.

"I know you are curious to see what we all came up with. Well here is your uncensored list of brainstormed ideas for generating 15 million extra in the next six to 12 months. Please note that if any ideas were duplicated, only one shows up here."

- Sell 15 percent of stores off to franchisees for a 10 percent discount. Revenue: 20 million.
- Raise our selling prices by one percent. Revenue: six million.
- Borrow against assets for the full 15 million.
- Use the existing 10 million to generate the additional 15 million.
- Outsource advertising to an unknown, new company for half the price.
- Provide stock option incentives for franchises to increase sales.
- Cut executive salaries by 30 percent. (Applause)
- Eliminate all but 6,000 square feet of corporate office space and have company employees work remotely.
- Have all stores purchase local products, rather than centrally shipped brand products. Send out brand logo labels for cups, coffees etc.
- Outsource Accounting, HR and manufacturing divisions eliminating 20 percent of staff.
- Sell currently held shares.
- Sell a stock delivery package to all hospitals and large businesses, for example,

- 40 gallons of coffee, 400 pastries etc. with a two percent delivery fee. Sell these direct and take an extra one percent from the franchise for the sale (s).
- Rent out existing real estate holdings and place corporate operations in existing low-end offices with minimal renovation. Combine this with remote workers when possible.

The list went on to discuss various tax and investment strategies.

"Thank you everyone!" Amy Ann said. "We have generated some great ideas today. Please be prepared to huddle on one or more of these in your own groups over the next few months. We'll be in touch!"

With that, Amy Ann walked into the crowd, shaking hands with many of the participants. Her demeanor was relaxed and suggested completion. She had come a long way from the temp receptionist with the diamond nose stud.

Not only Amy Ann, but the entire company had begun to breathe, it seemed, with the sharing of ideas and the tacit message from the executive decision-makers, "Your input is valuable and we take it seriously."

As she left the room, Miles hurried to catch up with Amy Ann. "Say, are you going to be around next month at the Town Meeting?"

Amy Ann nodded absently. "Yes…I will be there. It's our first one."

"OK. Well, I wanted to talk to you about something. Maybe we could have lunch beforehand?"

"OK."

"At Jules's"

"Sure. I'll meet you there at 11:30."

"It's a plan, Stan," Miles jogged ahead and waved. "Gotta go!"

Amy Ann watched him retreat and felt she already knew what he had to say.

YOUR PERFECT STORM

The Emerald Big Top Circus tours for five months out of the year. The home base is in Hollywood, Florida, where they house their animals and train new employees.

Recently, ticket sales have been very low, making it difficult to travel with the full retinue of five elephants, three tigers, two lions, eight chimpanzees, props, tents, concessions and 40 performers and maintenance people. That's a lot of trailers, buses, trucks and special equipment. The circus needs to make $100,000 per performance, and in the last year they averaged $89,000 or less. Tickets sell at large booking houses for $30 to $60 apiece.

What can The Emerald Big Top Circus do to make their revenue this year, without traveling as much to their usual destinations along the Eastern seaboard and then down along the Mississippi and back home?

Chapter 19

Build a Business Culture for Innovation Brainstorming

"Bosses are always surprised at how much knowledge exists further down the ladder."

ROBERT THIRKELL, CREATIVE DIRECTOR, THE BBC
FROM THE ARTICLE: DOWN THE UP STAIRCASE

Class Act
by Will Bullas, with permission of the artist. www.willbullas.com

Customers buy based on differences, not sameness. So how does a company cultivate a climate for continual innovation through brainstorming?

My answer: Encourage new, different, and even weird ideas. The culture must accept failures (temporary), but not accept an unwillingness to try new ideas. Idea generation and innovation brainstorming can become a regular part of discussions and meetings, both impromptu and regularly scheduled.

Foster an innovation culture in which innovation brainstorming is a natural part of life at work. This requires those in managerial positions to relinquish a tight rein on hierarchy. I say this because; the openness to try new ideas means openness to mistakes, without punishment or blame. All employees need to feel that they can suggest a new idea without fear of demotion or criticism. In fact, suggesting new ideas can become part of a performance evaluation.

Fostering an innovation culture also means investing in the time and space to allow brainstorming to occur. When your team needs a fresh outlook - and you can afford the time and expense - go to a different location, somewhere off-site. It is also great to just move to a different space within your own building. Here are a few possibilities:

1. Change your setting.
   - It could be that a single large table is exchanged for small team tables.
   - You might bring in an unusual snack and decorate the room in a theme.
   - You might invite a different group of participants than the usual team.
   - How about having the meeting outside at a picnic table with benches, of course, weather permitting?
   - Reserve a classroom in a nearby college.

2. Build a special room that encourages creativity and innovation brainstorming. Paint it different colors from the corporate choices. Fill it with comfortable chairs, rugs so you can sit on the floor, and tables that can be re-arranged easily. Arrange lots of fun and colorful items around the room. Hang interesting artwork or posters that encourage innovation. There are companies that specialize in designing "innovation" rooms.

The best ideas come from cutting across disciplines and looking into fields that are far from your own.

Cross-functional views also work well. For example, ask yourself: "If I were an artist, (or a teacher, a doctor, a scientist, a movie director, a movie actor, my mother, my grandfather or a child) how would I view this?"

View the same question or topic from viewpoint of other types of intelligence. Change your perspective by asking "what if?" questions.

State what the rules are, and then challenge the rules.

Investigate the assumptions that you have, and then decide which assumptions you can drop.

What metaphors apply to your problem, situation or question?

What is humorous about this? What strange juxtapositions can you see?

Always come up with several ideas as different as possible from each other before settling on one solution.

How could you adapt something that already exists?

Innovation is seeing old things in new ways, seeing connections between ideas not before connected, seeing new ways to use something that already exists. Innovation means little changes and improvements, as well as radical shifts. Each idea is a stepping-stone to more ideas.

The poet, Robert Frost said, "*I took the path less traveled and that has made all the difference.*"

To foster innovation in your company regularly arrange to have teams of people in a room, each person with a different background, education, experience, and thinking style. The combination will produce many more diverse ideas than one person thinking with paper and pen or even with a computer.

For example, Quadrant D people (Big Picture) find it easier to try and fail and try again. Quadrant B people (Organized) want to get more data before taking the step. They need to feel surer of success before stepping forward.

A	**D**
Rational	**Experimental/ Big picture**
What's the Bottom line, just the facts?	What will the result look like?
What needs to get done?	Why are we doing this?
How much risk?	Who will benefit?
How do we get on with it?	How many options are available?
Quick decisions	Decisions with options
Debates	Throws out more choices
B	**C**
Safekeeping, Organized	**Interpersonal**
What's the bottom line - data, proof?	How do we build the right team?
What details, what reduces risk?	Who should be on the team?
How and when must steps be taken?	Who will be impacted?
Careful decisions	Comfortable, stable decisions
Defends	Supports the team decision

Make it company policy to articulate this idea at every opportunity: ***Failure serves an important learning purpose.*** We learn more from our failure than from our successes. Sometimes we feel we have made a mistake. Figure out what happened, learn to avoid that mistake in the future and move on. Sometimes it is a more pervasive problem. Here too, it is necessary to understand, fix it, learn from what happened, and move on.

If something you are trying isn't going to work, you want it to fail as fast and inexpensively as possible. Again, learn from it and move on. Ideally, you already have metrics set up in your business that you use to measure whether or not an innovation was a success. I would caution you, however, that creative ideas need time to flourish and to be tweaked. Taking a rigid, linear approach to trying new ideas may have you scrap real profit generators without realizing it.

Ask: "What is best case? What is worst case?"

Instead of asking, "What is wrong with this idea?" ask, "What is right?, or "Where could it be applied?", or "Who would like it?"

Look at it upside down and backwards,

Charles Darwin's theories of evolution were all based on the fact that nature caused mutations and changes, and the "fittest" would survive to pass on the changes to their offspring. The ones that didn't work out would not survive. Observe how that is happening with products, services, processes, and ideas in your industry and your organization.

When fostering innovation around product development and design ask:

- Who would want it?
- What could they do with it?
- Why would they choose it?
- What if the design was more attractive?
- What if it was smaller? Bigger?
- Where would they expect to be able to buy it?
- What type of service would they expect?
- How can we produce faster?
- When are our prospects most ready for what we offer?

Let ideas mellow in your mind, sleep on it. When we dream, anything is possible, --nothing feels strange or out of place. That is why many ideas come to us in dreams.

Leadership for Innovation Brainstorming

The bottom line is that brainstorming, or a culture of innovation in a company, generates profits. As profit margins shrink with spiraling taxes, insurance and energy costs, new profits lie in using the imagination and initiative of people to creatively impact the market.

People who are used to doing what they're told and conforming to a mold may need some prodding and leadership to expand into an innovation culture.

Brainstorming, creativity, and innovation is not just about new products or offers, it is about solving problems, developing new methods and processes, and doing whatever you do in new and better ways. It is about iterative changes and many small improvements.

Leaders can model a non-judgmental, flat hierarchy as much as possible. They can encourage new ideas in and out of brainstorming sessions by actually implementing suggestions. They can make a point of talking about their own business failures and what they learned from them.

Finally, leaders have to make the time and space for groups to brainstorm. In the end, an innovation culture is a result of leaders acting creatively and without fear of losing control.

Problem-Solving in The Open Brainstorming Culture

Brainstorming and generating new ideas is as important for your day-to-day business problem-solving as it is for generating new product ideas and other more traditional applications. When you solve problems by pushing beyond the first answer to come up with to the best answers you can find, you will be rewarded every day with ROI, Return on Investment and Return on Ideas.

 STORM SESSION 16

Under the gently billowing silk of the large outdoor tent, all of the company employees either sat or stood or milled around, talking with friends. On the perimeters were representatives from different restaurants, offering samples of their best new dishes.

It was a beautiful late summer day, and the mood was relaxed and peaceful.

Gradually a hush fell over the crowd as Arjun Bux, Theo Wilson and Madeline Gegoux stood before the crowd. With them was a fourth person, Elmer Johnston, the CEO of the company. Elmer took the microphone.

"Everyone, I'm glad to see that you're enjoying the food. There's plenty, so don't be shy about going back for seconds," he chuckled amiably. "Arjun, Theo and Madeline have been telling me stories about your brainstorming sessions. I myself have come to rely on the ideas you are generating."

"As a step towards making this company more innovation-friendly, I'd like to say to each one of you, 'thank you.' Thank you for contributing above and beyond with your creative ideas. Some of you have contributed over and over again, taxing your brains and your bodies to come up with out-of-the-box solutions."

"We've put many of your ideas into motion. For instance, we shot a YouTube video of a band playing a song that meshes with our brand message and posted that video with a short voice-over tag line all over the news and entertainment sites on the Internet."

"We've brought in many different types of community bonding activities into our stores, such as a physical (as opposed to virtual) bulletin boards for singles, as well as silent films for senior demographics."

"Some of the ideas that we've tried have failed, like celebrity visits, wheat grass shots and dance lessons." He chuckled again. "To tell you the truth, trying these ideas was an enormous learning experience. I would do it again."

He paused emphatically. "I believe that this company is on the verge of something unprecedented. I have a feeling in my bones that with a culture of creative innovation, we can not only regain our market share, but break all records every year from now on."

"Let us all bear with ourselves and one another as we learn to let ourselves fall, get back up, learn to listen to each other and, most importantly, learn to say out loud new ideas without censoring them or worrying that they may be weird, wrong or stupid."

The employees broke out in to wild cheers, and many blew noisemakers.

Miles stood next to Amy at the edge of the tent.

"Aren't you going to miss this?" She asked him.

He shook his head. "Nah. We'll have our own company culture. We'll have Town Meetings too, you know. G.Q.'s all for brainstorming as a company culture."

"I guess pool halls need as much innovation as coffee shops do," she smiled.

"We do, we do. In fact, more, because you know, people sometimes have a wrong image of pool halls, and we have to help them see that we're family oriented."

"Maybe you could stage a theatrical production of *The Music Man* to launch your pool halls," Amy Ann suggested laughing.

"See! That is exactly the kind of brainstorming ideas that we need!" Miles pulled out his cell phone and spoke into the memo feature, "Produce musical, *The Music Man* as a launch."

Amy Ann watched him affectionately. Without warning, she kissed him on the cheek.

"I guess I'll see you later."

Miles blushed and nodded. "Saturday, six p.m. I will pick you up. The show starts at 7:30, so we will have plenty of time to eat dinner, I think."

"It's a date." Amy Ann took her leave, waving happily as she was called forward by Theo to take the microphone and lead the crowd in a chorus of "American Pie" (and coffee).

When the song was over, Elmer stepped back up to the microphone. "During our first company "Town Meeting," Theo, Arjun, Madeline and I are all ready to listen to your feedback. Each of us will be moving to a different section and sitting in an informal circle. Please come and engage in the conversations that we're having. Your feedback and suggestions surrounding everything from management, to sales and of course product…your feedback is literally gold to us. Someone will be at each circle just to transcribe what you have to say, so that it won't be lost. This isn't about keeping your thoughts to yourself. Even if you have some critical remarks, please share them!"

Elmer laughed again, his eyes full of good humor. "I personally promise you that no one will be singled out in any way for being critical."

The group of listening employees seemed both thrilled and dismayed at their CEO's announcement. Gradually, a few dozen people drifted over to the circles and began sharing ideas.

The sun was falling below the horizon before Elmer, Theo, Arjun and Madeline finally shook hands and called it a day. They had heard some startling comments. They had been challenged, even angered, but as the four of them reconvened briefly in Elmer's office, they all agreed that they were onto something. Theo summed it up, "I'm a little pissed off at some of the criticisms I heard today, but I have to say that I feel a level of energy – a life flowing in this company that I've never really felt before. Ultimately, I think it can only be a good thing."

Elmer sat down in his desk chair and looked up at the others. "Until tonight, I really wasn't sure about this change. I…It's been a big change, I can tell you from the way we used to do things. But after tonight, after hearing so many people say that they finally feel excited and heard. Well, all I can say is, 'I'm in.'"

He looked at each person. "Thank you. I'm grateful to you all for the hard work of listening. Let's look at the compilation of ideas and meet again on Tuesday."

Everyone said their goodbyes and left the office. Soon the building was dark and quiet, the tent rolled away on a truck with the tables.

YOUR PERFECT STORM

Please list three experiences of failure you have had in your life in relation to business. What did you learn from these experiences? How do you feel about trying something new and untried now?

Write down three new actions you are willing to take that could result in failure, but could also result in success.

Do you need approval to try these things? If so, how easy or difficult will it be to get your team or manager to buy into your idea?

Discuss three ways that your company could foster a culture of creative innovation.

Chapter 20

Epilogue: What You Have Gained

Now you know that there is no problem, no question too small or too big that cannot be turned inside out and either solved or transformed completely into an entirely new problem and question.

The practice of brainstorming relies primarily upon three ingredients:

1. An open company culture that allows for failure and questioning.
2. An established place and structure for practicing brainstorming.

This includes:
   a. A Facilitator
   b. A room or meeting place conducive to creative thinking
   c. Adherence to the rules of working fast and showing no judgment of one's own or of others' ideas.
3. Engaged people willing to let out their creative side.

I have mentioned some basic techniques of brainstorming for you that will stand you in good stead as you tackle thorny questions: mind mapping, clustering, whole brained thinking, diversity and the quadrant of intelligences.

When a business enterprise takes brainstorming seriously they have found the hidden door that leads to the underground river of expanding profits, employee fulfillment and customer satisfaction. Stay with it, even if it feels uncomfortable at first. In a short time, you will find yourself relying on your own ingenuity and that of your colleagues, as a reliable business resource.

What happened with the coffee shop company and our band of brainstormers?

Amy Ann made brainstorming Facilitator her career. She learned a thing or two about business operations in the process and went on to become a speaker and seminar leader on the subject. This was after her marriage to Miles, of course.

G.Q. and Miles built up their pool hall business, and then G.Q. left to travel the pro pool circuit. He started wearing gabararas instead of sweater vests and reading fiction instead of history. He stayed loyal to his various war reenactments, forfeiting a major pool tournament once so that he could return to Virginia for the staging of a key battle.

Anthony remained very happy in his job and with the company. He spent the next 13 years contributing his ideas and skills to make it one of the most successful and competitive franchise operations in the world.

Julia moved into the audio/video production department of marketing and learned more about American culture, in the process of making corporate films, than she ever imagined. One morning, she found herself humming that old Shaker song, "…turn, turn, turn 'til we come round right."

Smitty stayed with electricity, for which he had a passion, and eventually he bought a couple of acres, backing up to public parklands, and a mobile home. He built up a stable of horses with careful barters and trades and finally left the coffee shop company to lead rides and do freelance electrical work.

Daisy, like Anthony, stayed in her job as designer and committed herself to supporting a culture of openness and creativity. In fact, Daisy sometimes facilitated brainstorming sessions when the acting Facilitator couldn't make it or there were two sessions at the same time.

Georgia stepped in when Amy Ann left. She was about 70 at that point and had a wit that crackled like a warm fire. She let her hair go entirely white and styled it into a short, spiky do. She traded her pumps for designer running shoes and took on the task of whipping her colleagues into innovative jamborees with great pride.

Chapter 21

Bonus Exercises

"Do not go where the path may lead, go instead where there is no path and leave a trail."

~ RALPH WALDO EMERSON

On Your Own

1. Use this problem for practice or choose something you've been struggling with for a while. How can I use my three weeks total of vacation time to result in as much quality time with my family and still come back feeling rested and relaxed?
    a. List all the options you can think of, making sure the number is over 25.
    b. Divide the options among the family members who can read and write up to a maximum of five from your list, preferably ones that are quite different from each other. Have each one come up with at least 25 more ideas without repeating any of the five they received.
    c. When you get all the ideas back, do a mind map or cluster diagram including all the ideas even some that you think are too silly or too expensive or not possible. Combine and note repeats.
    d. Choose the top three to explore for cost and possibilities.
2. How can I plan my sales calls so that I minimize travel time and maximize the time I have in front of customers and prospects?
3. Pick a book on the topic you are working on and randomly choose 10 page numbers and a number for the line on the page. Then, use the line from each page as the inspiration for ideas. Come up with five items from each line. Some may be a stretch, based on only one word, others may follow naturally. Some may just be where your thinking went off on a tangent because of something in that line of prose.
4. Write a story about a stray dog that wanders into your place of business and give it three different endings.
5. Use mind mapping to plan your next meeting. This can be done whether you are the leader of the meeting who will plan the agenda or a participant who would like to accomplish some particular results. Include the names of everyone who will be there and what you expect them to need and to contribute.
6. Think about a problem that never seems to get fixed around the house. Maybe it is something that you've done quick repairs that don't last long; maybe it's something you haven't gotten around to. Make a list of 12 barriers to getting this problem fixed once and for all. After you

have 12 (or more), go down the list and write how to get around every one of those barriers.

7. Tackling your assumptions: There are so many things in life that we think we know but may be based on an assumption rather than proof. Sometimes that is because it is a subject that can't be proven. It can only present itself many times to us in the same manner or guise, so that we start to assume it will always be that way. Take the next 24 hours and pay close attention to everything you day and write. Stop and ask yourself, could this be an assumption? Say to yourself, "How do I know that?" If you don't remember how you came to that conclusion, meaning that you don't have proof, how would you get proof or disprove it? List at least five ways you could determine whether or not it is an assumption.

With A Team

1. Develop a mission statement for your team.
2. Plan a celebration if your team exceeds all its goals for the year. How can you do something you've never done as a group before and that everyone will enjoy?
3. List the top 10 strategies for success in what your team does. First, each person on their own needs to list 20 strategies. Then organize them into categories and work together to prioritize.
4. Develop a plan to achieve positive word of mouth buzz about your next new product or service. What are all the ways you can create reasons for customers and prospects to talk about your company? Don't limit yourself by costs or what you might initially think are hurdles or difficulties.
5. You own a company that sells a variety of products and are feeling pressure to discount. All your competitors are in a pricing war, and it threatens to pull your company into the war. You realize that will be a losing battle. So instead, brainstorm, using any of the tools or techniques in this book, to come up with ways that would make your customers fiercely loyal.
6. Pick the toughest problem your team has been grappling with in the last few months that either has not been solved or has not been solved well. Work together to list 20 barriers to getting that problem solved

well, once and for all. Some on the list not everyone will agree with but if anyone feels it is a barrier, then it should be on the list. Then go back through the list and come up with a way to overcome each of the barriers.

7. Every project, every problem, and every issue your team needs to tackle starts with some facts (things you know you know, that you can prove), some assumptions (things your team thinks they know, but have no proof), and some things they don't know, but need to know. Start the next brainstorming session with three columns: Facts, Assumptions, Need to Know

FACTS	ASSUMPTIONS	NEED TO KNOW

8. So often at work we put measurements in place about revenue, money, ROI (return on investment) and other numbers that relate directly to counting the cash. While not minimizing the importance of cash flow, spend some time on the next brainstorming project thinking only about ways to save:
    - Time
    - Customers' time
    - Employees' time
    - Management's time
    - Time to complete a new product or service development
    - Time to get to work
    - Design time

    Make sure you brainstorm long enough to get plenty of ideas on the list, using any of the techniques in this book. You may find that the ROI (Return on Ideas) for saving time will make a measurable difference that can even be translated back into money.

Resources

Additional Material, Reading and Brainstorming Tools

"If the only tool you have is a hammer, everything will look like a nail"

UNKNOWN

Definitions

Thinking Style Quadrants:

A. Blue Quadrant: Rational	**D. Yellow Quadrant: Big picture**
Bottom line: facts	Creative
Logical	Explores
Quick decisions	Wants lots of options
Quick to change decisions when necessary	Likes change for its own sake
Task oriented	People oriented
Takes on risk	Multitasks most things
Impatient	Imaginative
Demanding	Focuses on the future
Stops listening if not immediately relevant	Big goals
Focuses on today, the present	Easily thinks in the abstract
Competitive	Influencing
Strong ego	Generous
Practical goals	Speaks with emotion
Can think in the abstract	
B. Green Quadrant: Organized	**C. Red Quadrant: Inter-personal**
Safe-keeping	Team builder
Bottom line: data	Team Player
Detailed	Loyal
Critical	Focuses on the past for comfort
Competent	People oriented
Conscientious	Empathetic
Sequential, linear	Goes along with the team's decisions
Risk averse	Group goals
Task oriented	Patient
Careful decisions	Friendly
Defends decisions	Family oriented
Focuses on the past for proof & data	Reluctant to express contrary opinions
Plans in detail	Prefers to have direct experience, concrete
Specific goals	
Likes to think in concrete terms	

Intelligence Types

This is based on the groundbreaking work done by Howard Gardner and Daniel Goleman. Their research, along with others who have followed in their path, has shown that there are a number of different ways in which not only intelligence, but genius, can manifest itself in human beings and in the way the brain develops and works. If you agree with their conclusions, you start to see how the concept of Intelligence Quotient (IQ) only measures one or two of the intelligences possible. Gardner also theorizes and gives examples to illustrate that some people can have one type of intelligence that is much higher than all the others, or may cross over to more than one. Here we are suggesting that increasing the variety of intelligences exhibited on your team is a type of diversity that improves brainstorming results. Below is just a quick summary. See Multiple Intelligences or other books by Howard Gardner for more information and Emotional Intelligence by Daniel Goleman.

Linguistic
   Ability with language arts, verbal and written expression, communication of all types

Logical-Mathematical
   Ability in math and science, logic, reasoning,

Musical
   Ability to hear notes and tones, ability to create music

Bodily-kinesthetic
   Ability in sports, athletics, strength, flexibility,

Spatial
   Ability to understand, visualize, and design shapes, buildings, and items in their mind before they are formed.

Interpersonal – Social Intelligence
   Ability to establish rapport and trust, read body language and tone of voice, recognize crowd emotions and individual's emotions, alliance building.

Intrapersonal – Emotional Intelligence
   Ability to manage one's own emotions to fit any situation

One more note: Gardner does not believe there is an 'artistic intelligence' which would then be number 8. Instead he describes the artist as someone who uses particular intelligence(s) in an aesthetic way. An example he gives is the application of spatial intelligence can be used in a practical way as a surgeon or aesthetically as a sculptor or painter.

Brainstorming and Business Styles

Research going at least as far back as Carl Jung (1875-1961, a Swiss psychiatrist and colleague of Freud), and supported by MRI and CT Scans of the brain, have shown that people have significant differences in the way we make decisions, think, communicate and receive communication, and establish preferences.

Since first espoused by Jung, many psychologists and researchers have tried to come up with easier ways to describe those differences and develop assessments. The Myers-Briggs team of mother and daughter developed a well documented and validated assessment called the MBTI® (Myers-Briggs Type Instrument®) and called the 16 categories that resulted, different types. Ned Herrmann developed one at General Electric as part of the executive management team and later took it outside G.E. He formed a company and created an assessment tool he called the HBDI® (Herrmann Brain Dominance Instrument®).

What do the many validated assessments measure and how are they different?

Ann Herrmann-Nehdi, CEO of Herrmann International says it this way: *"Years ago when my father developed the Herrmann Brain Dominance Instrument® (HBDI®) at GE, other assessments existed (e.g. DiSC™ and MBTI®). Why develop another? Each assessment measures different things! MBTI® measures psychological preference (based on Carl Jung's work) and DiSC™ measures behavioral preference. My father was interested in thinking and learning preference, so he turned to brain research as the foundational premise of the HBDI® assessment. We learn different things from each approach. Extensive research and testing goes into validating an assessment so that decisions and interpretation can be based on the data it provides."*

To try the HBDI® assessment, go to www.hbdi.com (and let them know Hazel Wagner sent you). Or you can contact me directly.

Whether you call these different styles, preferences, types, or dominances, they are all similar in that they help us identify how we are different in our approach to life, business, thinking, and communication. Knowing how to identify those differences helps us recognize why and how communication and business relationships (and also personal relationships) can go wrong – sometimes to our complete surprise.

Though Myers-Briggs divides their types into 16 categories, most of the other style assessments use four divisions. For the purpose of this book use the four quadrant diagrams to choose one that you think describes you best. Those descriptions will help you guess your style and start you thinking about the styles of the people with whom you work. There is no good or bad style, no one style is better than another, and the best brainstorming sessions as well as the best chances for creativity and innovation come from having a diversity of styles on your team. Also, no one is all one style. We all have elements from each of the four quadrants. We usually have one or two quadrants that are more descriptive of our personal style than the others.

If you would like to get a more specific and complete description and evaluation, consider taking one of the assessments mentioned in this book. You can contact me to be able to try any one of the assessments mentioned in this book.

Reference Material

My web sites and blog will continue to add more resources and links to keep you up-to-date on these resources.
www.brainstorming-that-works.com
www.hazelwagner.com
www.brainiance.com
www.b9d.com
www.powerbrainstorming.com

Products

1. Thinkpak® from Michael Michalko, www.creativethinking.net
2. Knowbrainer® from SolutionPeople www.solutionpeople.com
3. Creative WhackPack® and Innovative WhackPack® from Roger von Oech www.creativethink.com

Web sites

1. www.brainstorming-that-works.com
2. www.visualthesaurus.com
3. All the software companies listed below have websites

Note: All of the following programs have been used in the development of this book and my Web site. They are extremely helpful when you want to use a mind map in a presentation or just want to share or work with others on the same mind map. There are links to all of the programs from my web site www.brainstorming-that-works.com and some of the links get you free trial versions, special offers or discounts.

Software

1. Novamind® from Novamind (Windows and MAC)
2. IMindMap™ from Tony Buzan (Windows and MAC)
3. Mindmanager® from Mindjet (Windows and MAC)
4. Mindgenius® from MindGenius (Windows only)
5. Flash brainer®, podbrainer®, and innovation activator from Solution-People
6. ConceptDraw®
7. ThoughtOffice® by Mark Allan Effinger (based on IdeaFisher)
8. IdeaFisher® by Marsh Fisher (Century 21 Founder)

More Reading

1. *Business Guide to Mind Mapping* by Gideon King
2. *Thinkertoys* by Michael Michalko
3. *Change Your Thinking, Change Your Life* by Edelstein & Steele
4. *Thinking for a Change* by John Maxwell
5. *Frames of Mind. The Theory of Multiple Intelligences*, Howard Gardner's classic work
6. *Think Like Leonardo da Vinci or Your Genius* by Michael Gelb
7. *The Creative Brain* by Ned Herrmann
8. *The Whole Brain Business Book* by Ned Herrmann
9. *A Whole New Mind* by Daniel Pink
10. *Whack on the Side of Head* by Roger von Oech
11. *Tipping Point* and *Blink* by Malcolm Gladwell
12. *Brain Power* by Karl Albrecht
13. *6 Thinking Hats* (and many others) by Edward de Bono
14. *The Brain that Changes Itself* by Norman Doidge
15. *Frames of Mind and Multiples Intelligences: The Theory in Practice* by Howard Gardner
16. *The Mind Map Book and Mind Mapping for Kids* (and many more) by Tony Buzan

Workbooks

Teacher's Guide to Mind Mapping by Gideon King
How to Think like Leonardo da Vinci Workbook by Michael Gelb
Mapping Inner Space by Nancy Margulies

Assessments

1. HBDI® Herrmann Brain Dominance Instrument®
   Herrmann International
   794 Buffalo Creek
   Lake Lure NC 28746
   USA
   1-828-625-9153
   1-800-432-4234 (in USA and Canada)
   www.HBDI.com

2. Myers-Briggs
   CPP
   3803 Bayshore Road
   Palo Alto, CA 94303
   1-800-642-1765
   www.cpp.com

3. DISC
   American Management Association
   1601 Broadway
   New York, NY 10019
   www.amanet.org

4. DISC Extended
   Extended DISC North America, Inc.
   1.800.257.7481
   www.extendeddisc.com/north_america
   info.usa@extendeddisc.com
   info.canada@extendeddisc.com

5. Mindex
   Karl Albrecht International
   MAIN#: 858-576-3535 (PST, USA) / FAX#: 858-576-3536
   Web site: http://www.KarlAlbrecht.com

---

[1] Copyright 2001-2009 Herrmann International adapted by Hazel Wagner The four color four quadrant graphic is a trademark of Herrmann International.

Notes and Credits

Credits

Photographs and images supplied and copyrighted by artist & fotolia
- Prologue © Jeffrey Collingwood
- Chapter 1 © Stephen Coburn
- Chapter 2 © Scott Maxwell and ©Gehirn von der Seit
- Chapter 3 © Kreego
- Chapter 5 © V. Yakobchuk
- Chapter 9 © ktsdesign
- Chapter 12 © Alexey Shestakov
- Chapter 18 © Stephen Coburn
- Chapter 20 © Mario Ragma Jr.
- Chapter 21 © Tomasz Trojanowski

Paintings by and copyright owner Will Bullas, with permission of the artist, www.willbullas.com
- Chapter 4 Higher Learning
- Chapter 6 Monkey Business
- Chapter 7 Does a Bear Think in the Woods
- Chapter 8 A Square Pig in a Round Hole
- Chapter 10 The Mediator
- Chapter 11 A Meeting of the Minds
- Chapter 13 Cats and Dogma
- Chapter 15 Jesters Do Often Prove Prophets
- Chapter 17 Fridays After Five
- Chapter 19 Class Act

Notes:

Chapter 2
Invented by Harry Greene, Dentist designed and manufactured by Hans Freeman (my father), Creative Plastics Engineering Co.

Chapter 3
Forest and trees mind-maps developed using IMindMap™ from Tony Buzan.

Chapter 5
[1] Herrmann Brain Dominance Instrument ® is a registered trademark of Herrmann International and the term is used with written permission thereof.
[2] Based on the HBDI® and other formal assessment attributes
[3] (*Scientific American* magazine, "The Memory Code", July 2007)
[4] E.G., HBDI®, Mindex, DISC
[5] More information on http://www. brainstorming-that-works.com and http://www.cpp.com/products/mbti/index.asp
[6] Herrmann Brain Dominance Instrument®, developed originally at General Electric by Ned Herrmann, www.hdbi.com or www.brainiance.com
[7] Copyright 2001-09 Herrmann International adapted by Hazel Wagner

Chapter 8
[1] Mind map made using MindManager™ by Mindjet

Chapter 9
[1] 'Whole brained' is a trademark registered by Herrmann International

Chapter 10
[1] Based on any of the popular thinking style instruments or techniques (e.g., DISC, Mindex, Myers-Briggs MBTI®, HBDI®)

Chapter 11
[1] This and other Einstein quotes from http://www.einstein-quotes.com

Chapter 12
[1] See the Resource section at the end of the book for these definitions.
[2] These mind maps were made using Novamind™: www.novamind.com

Chapter 13
[1] See the list of mind mapping programs in the resource section at the end of this book.
[2] A type of Mexican cheese

Chapter 14
[1] Mind map made using Novamind™ www.novamind.com
[2] Mind map made using MindManager™ from Mindjet www.mindjet.com
[3] Mind map made using IMindMap™ www.imindmap.com

Chapter 15
[1] Cluster diagram developed using the fast brainstorming tool in the ConceptDraw mind mapping software.

Chapter 16
[1] These Forest and Trees mind-maps were made using the Novamind™ software program. www.novamind.com
[2] Originally developed by Yasuo Matsumura of Clover Management Research in Chiba City, Japan

Chapter 18
[1] Mind-map made using MindJet's MindManager www.mindjet.com
[2] Copyright 2001-2009 Herrmann International adapted by Hazel Wagner
[3] Copyright 2001-2009 Herrmann International adapted by Hazel Wagner The four color four quadrant graphic is a trademark of Herrmann International.

Chapter 19
[1] Copyright 2001-2009 Herrmann International adapted by Hazel Wagner The four color four quadrant graphic is a trademark of Herrmann International.

www.ingramcontent.com/pod-product-compliance
Lightning Source LLC
Chambersburg PA
CBHW030139170426
43199CB00008B/132